Real Estate Wealth

Strategies for Successful Investment

RICHARD J. MILLS

1

Table of contents

2

3

INTRODUCTION

THE POWER OF REAL ESTATE INVESTMENT

Real estate investment has long been recognized as a powerful and lucrative avenue for wealth creation. With its ability to generate passive income, provide long-term appreciation, and offer a variety of investment strategies, real estate has captured the attention of seasoned investors and newcomers alike.

The power of real estate investment lies in its potential to build wealth over time. Unlike other investment vehicles such as stocks or bonds, real estate offers tangible assets that can appreciate in value and generate income simultaneously.

Whether it's residential properties, commercial buildings, or even vacant land, real estate investments can provide a stable and consistent cash flow that grows over time.

One of the key advantages of real estate investment is the ability to leverage. Through the use of financing options like mortgages, investors can acquire properties with a fraction of the total purchase price, thereby magnifying their return on investment. This leverage allows individuals to control assets worth significantly more than their initial capital investment, potentially amplifying their profits.

4

Moreover, real estate investment offers diversification benefits. Adding real estate to an investment portfolio can help mitigate risk by spreading it across different asset classes. Real estate values often move independently of stock market fluctuations, making it a valuable hedge against market volatility.

Additionally, real estate investment provides tax advantages that can enhance overall returns. Deductible expenses such as mortgage interest, property taxes, and depreciation can significantly reduce the tax burden on rental income, ultimately increasing the profitability of the investment.

Furthermore, real estate offers multiple investment strategies to suit various goals and risk tolerances. Investors can choose to buy and hold properties for long-term appreciation, flip properties for quick profits, or engage in rental property investments for ongoing cash flow. These diverse strategies allow investors to tailor their approach based on their financial objectives and personal preferences.

It is important to note that real estate investment requires careful research, analysis, and management. Market conditions, location, property maintenance, and tenant 5

management are just a few of the factors that can impact the success of a real estate investment. However, with the right knowledge, diligence, and guidance, real estate investment can be a powerful tool for building long-term wealth and financial security.

In conclusion, the power of real estate investment lies in its potential to generate passive income, provide long-term appreciation, offer diversification, leverage, tax advantages, and a range of investment strategies. With proper planning and execution, real estate investment can be a rewarding venture for investors looking to grow their wealth and secure their financial future.

6

CHAPTER ONE

UNDERSTANDING THE REAL ESTATE MARKET

The real estate market refers to the buying, selling, and renting of properties, including residential homes, commercial buildings, and land. Understanding the real estate market involves gaining knowledge about various factors that influence property values, market trends, and the dynamics of supply and demand.

Here are some key aspects to consider when seeking to understand the real estate market: Market Conditions: Real estate markets can vary from region to region and are influenced by factors such as the overall economy, interest rates, job growth, population demographics, and government policies. Monitoring these conditions can provide insights into the state of the market.

Property Valuation: Understanding how property values are determined is crucial. Factors such as location, property size, condition, amenities, and recent sales of similar properties in the area affect the value of a property. Appraisals and comparative market analysis reports can help assess property values.

7

Supply and Demand: The balance between the supply of available properties and the demand from buyers or renters has a significant impact on the real estate market. When supply exceeds demand, prices may decline, whereas when demand exceeds supply, prices tend to rise.

Market Trends: Following market trends is important for identifying opportunities and risks. Trends can include shifts in buyer preferences, development of new neighborhoods or commercial areas, and changes in property prices over time.

Analyzing historical data and tracking current market indicators can help identify trends.

Financing and Mortgage Rates: Mortgage interest rates and lending conditions influence buyers' purchasing power and affordability. Understanding financing options, mortgage rates, and lending practices can help gauge the market's strength and the level of buyer activity.

Real Estate Professionals: Consulting with real estate agents, brokers, or professionals specializing in market analysis can provide valuable insights. These professionals have experience and knowledge of local markets and can offer guidance on investment opportunities or the selling process.

8

Market Research: Conducting thorough research is crucial before making any real estate decisions. Analyzing data, market reports, economic forecasts, and local housing market statistics can provide a more comprehensive understanding of the real estate market.

Remember that real estate markets can be complex and dynamic, with local factors playing a significant role. It's important to stay informed, seek expert advice when needed, and consider long-term trends and factors that can influence the market's stability and growth.

ECONOMIC FACTORS AFFECTING REAL ESTATE

Introduction:

The real estate market is closely intertwined with the overall economy, and various economic factors significantly influence its dynamics. Understanding these economic factors is crucial for investors, homeowners, and industry professionals to make informed decisions.

9

This note explores the key economic factors that affect the real estate market and highlights their impact on property values, market conditions, and investment opportunities.

Interest Rates:

Interest rates have a substantial impact on the real estate market. Lower interest rates make borrowing more affordable, stimulating demand for properties. This can lead to increased home sales and higher property prices.

Conversely, higher interest rates can reduce affordability and slow down the market, potentially causing a decline in property values.

Economic Growth:

The overall economic growth of a region or country plays a significant role in the real estate market. During periods of robust economic growth, there is usually increased job creation, rising incomes, and greater consumer confidence.

This positive economic environment can drive up demand for real estate, resulting in higher property values and increased investment activity.

Employment and Wage Levels:

The availability of jobs and the strength of wage levels directly influence the real estate market. Low unemployment 10

rates and steady wage growth enhance purchasing power and contribute to a healthy housing market. Strong job markets attract people to specific areas, leading to increased demand for housing and potentially driving up property prices.

Supply and Demand:

Supply and demand dynamics have a direct impact on property values. In areas where the demand for housing exceeds the available supply, prices tend to rise. Conversely, when there is an oversupply of properties relative to demand, prices may decline. Economic factors such as population growth, demographic shifts, and construction activity all contribute to the supply and demand balance in the real estate market.

Consumer Confidence:

Consumer confidence reflects people's perceptions of the current and future state of the economy. When consumers feel optimistic about economic conditions, they are more likely to make significant purchases, including buying real estate. High consumer confidence boosts housing demand, strengthens the market, and can lead to price appreciation.

Government Policies and Regulations:

11

Government policies and regulations can significantly influence the real estate market. Policies related to taxation, zoning, interest rates, and lending practices can impact property values and investment decisions. For example, tax incentives for homeownership or favorable zoning regulations for commercial development can stimulate real estate activity and drive up property values.

Inflation:

Inflation refers to the general increase in prices over time.

While moderate inflation is often considered a sign of a healthy economy, it can affect the real estate market.

Inflation can lead to higher construction costs, increased material prices, and rising property values. Real estate is often seen as a hedge against inflation, as property values tend to appreciate over the long term.

Conclusion:

Economic factors play a critical role in shaping the real estate market. Interest rates, economic growth, employment levels, supply and demand dynamics, consumer confidence, government policies, and inflation all contribute to the overall health and performance of the real estate sector.

Understanding these factors and their interplay can help stakeholders make informed decisions, assess investment 12

opportunities, and navigate the ever-changing landscape of the real estate market.

Types of Real Estate Investments

Real Estate Market Analysis

TYPES OF REAL ESTATE INVESTMENTS:

Residential Properties: This includes single-family homes, townhouses, condominiums, and apartment buildings that are primarily used for residential purposes. Investors can buy properties and rent them out for regular income or sell them for capital appreciation.

Commercial Properties: These are properties used for business purposes, such as office buildings, retail stores, shopping malls, warehouses, and hotels. Investors can lease these properties to businesses, earning rental income.

Commercial real estate investments often offer higher returns but also involve higher risks.

13

Industrial Properties: Industrial properties are used for manufacturing, distribution, or storage purposes. They include factories, warehouses, industrial parks, and storage facilities. Industrial real estate can provide steady income from long-term leases with businesses.

Retail Properties: These properties are specifically designed for retail businesses, including standalone retail stores, strip malls, and shopping centers. Retail real estate investments can offer stable income through lease agreements with retailers.

Mixed-Use Properties: Mixed-use properties combine residential, commercial, and/or retail spaces in a single development. They can include apartments above retail stores, office spaces with ground-floor restaurants, or live/work units. These investments offer diversification and multiple income streams.

Real Estate Investment Trusts (REITs): REITs are companies that own, operate, or finance income-generating real estate.

Investors can buy shares in a publicly traded REIT, which allows them to invest in a diversified portfolio of properties without directly owning them. REITs offer regular dividends and liquidity.

14

Real Estate Development: This involves purchasing land or properties for the purpose of developing them into new residential, commercial, or mixed-use projects. Real estate developers seek to add value through construction, renovation, or redevelopment and then sell or lease the developed properties for profit.

REAL ESTATE MARKET ANALYSIS:

Real estate market analysis is the process of evaluating the current and future market conditions of a specific area or property to make informed investment decisions. *It involves analyzing various factors that can influence property values and demand, including:*

Supply and Demand: Assessing the balance between the number of available properties (supply) and the number of potential buyers or renters (demand) in the market. This helps determine the level of competition and the potential for price appreciation or rental income.

Economic Factors: Analyzing the overall economic conditions, such as GDP growth, employment rates, income 15

levels, and population trends. Strong economic fundamentals usually indicate a healthy real estate market.

Location: Evaluating the desirability of the location based on factors like proximity to amenities, schools, transportation, and employment centers. Prime locations often attract higher demand and command higher prices.

Market Trends: Monitoring market trends, such as price fluctuations, sales volume, rental rates, and vacancy rates.

This provides insights into the direction of the market and potential investment opportunities.

Regulatory and Legal Factors: Considering zoning regulations, building codes, permits, and any legal restrictions that may affect property development or investment.

Comparable Sales and Rental Analysis: Reviewing recent sales and rental data of similar properties in the area to assess property values, rental rates, and potential returns on investment.

Future Development and Infrastructure Plans: Examining planned developments, infrastructure projects, and 16

government initiatives that may impact property values and the overall market dynamics.

By conducting a comprehensive real estate market analysis, investors can make informed decisions about buying, selling, leasing, or developing properties, thereby maximizing their chances of success in the real estate market.

17

CHAPTER TWO

BUILDING A SOLID INVESTMENT STRATEGY

Introduction:

Developing a solid investment strategy is crucial for achieving long-term financial goals and building wealth. It involves careful planning, research, and analysis to make informed investment decisions.

This note provides a comprehensive guide to building a solid investment strategy.

Set Clear Financial Goals:

Before diving into investments, it is essential to define your financial goals. Determine what you want to achieve in the short term and long term. Common goals include saving for retirement, buying a house, funding education, or starting a business. Clear goals will help shape your investment strategy and provide a benchmark for measuring success.

Assess Risk Tolerance:

Understanding your risk tolerance is crucial in designing an investment strategy that aligns with your comfort level. Risk tolerance depends on factors such as age, financial situation, time horizon, and personal preferences. Generally, younger investors with a longer time horizon can afford to take more 18

risk, while older investors approaching retirement may prefer more conservative investments.

Diversify Your Portfolio:

Diversification is a key principle in investment strategy. It involves spreading investments across different asset classes, industries, and geographical regions. By diversifying, you reduce the risk of being overly exposed to a single investment. A diversified portfolio can include stocks, bonds, real estate, commodities, and alternative investments like hedge funds or private equity.

Conduct Thorough Research:

Research is essential for making informed investment decisions. Study the fundamentals of potential investments, including the company's financial health, management team, competitive position, and growth prospects. Use reliable sources of information such as financial statements, company reports, and analyst recommendations. Stay updated on market trends and economic indicators that can influence your investments.

Determine Asset Allocation:

Asset allocation refers to the percentage of your portfolio allocated to different asset classes. It is a crucial decision that 19

balances risk and potential returns. A common approach is to allocate a higher percentage to equities for long-term growth and a smaller portion to fixed-income assets for stability.

Adjust the asset allocation as you progress towards your financial goals or as market conditions change.

Monitor and Rebalance:

Regularly monitor your investments to ensure they are performing as expected and align with your investment strategy. Market fluctuations can cause your portfolio to deviate from the desired asset allocation. Rebalancing involves selling overperforming assets and reallocating funds to underperforming assets to maintain the desired balance.

This process ensures your portfolio stays in line with your risk tolerance and investment goals.

Consider Tax Efficiency:

Tax efficiency is an important aspect of any investment strategy. Understand the tax implications of your investments, such as capital gains taxes or dividends.

Explore tax-advantaged accounts like Individual Retirement Accounts (IRAs) or 401(k)s, which offer tax benefits.

Strategies like tax-loss harvesting can also help offset capital gains. Consult with a tax advisor to optimize your investment strategy from a tax perspective.

20

Stay Disciplined and Long-Term Oriented: Building wealth through investments is a long-term endeavor. Avoid making impulsive decisions based on short-term market fluctuations or emotions. Stick to your investment strategy and have patience. Keep a long-term perspective and focus on your financial goals. Regularly review and adjust your strategy as needed but avoid frequent and unnecessary changes that may hinder your progress.

Seek Professional Advice:

If you are unsure or overwhelmed, consider seeking professional advice from a financial advisor or investment professional. They can provide personalized guidance based on your specific circumstances, risk tolerance, and goals. An expert can help you navigate complex investment options, optimize your portfolio, and provide valuable insights.

Conclusion:

Building a solid investment strategy is a critical step towards achieving financial success. Set clear goals, assess your risk tolerance, diversify your portfolio, conduct thorough research, determine asset allocation, monitor and rebalance 21

SETTING INVESTMENT GOALS

Setting investment goals is an essential step in creating a well-defined investment strategy. Clear goals help you stay focused, measure progress, and make informed decisions.

Here are some key factors to consider when setting investment goals:

Time Horizon: Determine how long you plan to invest before needing the funds. Investment goals can be short-term (1-3

years), medium-term (3-10 years), or long-term (10+ years).

Your time horizon will influence your investment choices and risk tolerance.

Risk Tolerance: Assess your comfort level with market volatility and potential losses. Generally, risk and returns are correlated, so higher-risk investments may offer greater returns but also carry higher potential losses. Understanding your risk tolerance will help you choose appropriate investments.

Financial Objectives: Identify your specific financial objectives. These may include saving for retirement, purchasing a home, funding education, starting a business, or 22

achieving financial independence. Each objective will have a different time horizon and funding requirement.

Return Expectations: Consider the rate of return you expect to achieve on your investments. Historical data can provide a reference point, but keep in mind that past performance does not guarantee future results. Be realistic in setting your return expectations to align with your risk tolerance and the prevailing market conditions.

Diversification: Determine the level of diversification you want in your investment portfolio. Diversification involves spreading your investments across different asset classes (stocks, bonds, real estate, etc.) and sectors to reduce risk. It can help protect your portfolio from significant losses if one investment performs poorly.

Regular Contributions: Decide on the frequency and amount of contributions you can make to your investment portfolio.

Regular contributions, such as monthly or quarterly, help build your investments over time and can take advantage of dollar-cost averaging.

Tax Considerations: Understand the tax implications of your investment goals. Different investment vehicles have varying 23

tax treatments, such as tax-deferred retirement accounts or taxable brokerage accounts. Consider how taxes will impact your investment returns and overall financial plan.

Monitoring and Adjusting: Plan how frequently you will review and adjust your investment strategy. Regular monitoring allows you to evaluate progress toward your goals and make any necessary course corrections. However, avoid making impulsive changes based on short-term market fluctuations.

Remember, it's crucial to have realistic and achievable investment goals. They should be aligned with your financial situation, risk tolerance, and time horizon. Regularly reviewing and reassessing your goals will ensure they remain relevant as your circumstances evolve. Consider consulting with a financial advisor who can provide personalized guidance tailored to your specific needs and objectives.

RISK MANAGEMENT AND DIVERSIFICATION

Risk management and diversification are two important concepts in finance and investment. *Let's discuss each of them in detail:*

24

Risk Management:

Risk management refers to the process of identifying, assessing, and mitigating potential risks that may affect an individual, organization, or investment portfolio. The goal of risk management is to minimize the negative impact of uncertain events and protect against potential losses.

Some key principles of risk management include: a. Risk Identification: This involves identifying and understanding the various types of risks that may arise.

Common types of risks include market risk, credit risk, liquidity risk, operational risk, and legal risk.

b. Risk Assessment: Once risks are identified, they need to be assessed in terms of their potential impact and likelihood of occurrence. This helps in prioritizing risks and allocating resources accordingly.

c. Risk Mitigation: After assessing risks, appropriate measures are taken to mitigate or reduce them. This may involve implementing risk controls, diversifying investments, hedging strategies, or buying insurance.

25

d. Monitoring and Review: Risk management is an ongoing process. Risks should be continually monitored, and risk management strategies should be reviewed and adjusted as needed.

Diversification:

Diversification is a risk management technique that involves spreading investments across different assets, sectors, regions, or asset classes. The goal of diversification is to reduce the risk associated with investing in a single asset or a concentrated portfolio.

By diversifying investments, an investor can potentially reduce the impact of any one investment performing poorly.

If one investment underperforms, the gains from other investments may help offset the losses, resulting in a more stable and consistent overall return.

Diversification can be achieved in several ways: a. Asset Allocation: Allocating investments across different asset classes, such as stocks, bonds, real estate, and cash, helps spread risk and take advantage of different market conditions.

26

b. Sector Diversification: Investing in different sectors or industries can reduce the risk of being heavily exposed to the performance of a single sector. For example, diversifying between technology, healthcare, finance, and consumer goods sectors.

c. Geographic Diversification: Investing in different countries or regions helps reduce the risk associated with the performance of a specific country's economy or geopolitical events.

d. Investment Types: Diversification can also be achieved by investing in different types of securities, such as stocks, bonds, mutual funds, exchange-traded funds (ETFs), or alternative investments like commodities or real estate.

It's important to note that diversification does not guarantee profits or protect against all losses. It is still necessary to carefully analyze and select investments based on individual goals, risk tolerance, and investment horizon.

Overall, risk management and diversification are crucial elements in building a well-balanced investment portfolio, managing risk exposure, and increasing the potential for long-term success.

27

CREATING A REAL ESTATE PORTFOLIO

Creating a real estate portfolio involves strategically acquiring and managing a collection of properties for investment purposes.

Here are some steps to help you get started: Define your investment goals: Determine what you want to achieve with your real estate portfolio. Are you aiming for long-term capital appreciation, regular rental income, or a combination of both? Clarify your objectives to guide your investment decisions.

Assess your finances: Evaluate your current financial situation and determine how much capital you can allocate to real estate investments. Consider your risk tolerance, available funds, and potential financing options. Having a clear understanding of your financial position will help you set realistic investment targets.

Research the real estate market: Study the local and national real estate markets to identify areas with potential for growth and investment opportunities. Look for factors like population growth, economic development, infrastructure 28

projects, and job market stability. Analyze market trends and consult with local experts or real estate agents to gain insights into the market dynamics.

Determine your investment strategy: Decide on the types of properties you want to include in your portfolio. You can invest in residential properties, commercial properties, vacation rentals, or a mix of different property types.

Consider factors such as location, property size, rental demand, and potential returns when selecting properties.

Conduct thorough due diligence: Before purchasing a property, perform detailed research and analysis. Evaluate the property's condition, market value, rental potential, expenses, and any legal or regulatory considerations. Inspect the property, review its financial records, and assess its income-generating potential.

Develop a financing plan: Determine how you will finance your real estate investments. Explore options like traditional mortgages, private lenders, partnerships, or real estate investment trusts (REITs). Carefully consider the terms, interest rates, and repayment plans to ensure they align with your investment strategy and financial goals.

29

Diversify your portfolio: Spread your investments across different properties and locations to reduce risk.

Diversification helps protect your portfolio from fluctuations in a single market or property type. Consider investing in both high-growth and stable markets to balance risk and potential returns.

Property acquisition and management: Once you identify suitable properties, negotiate the purchase price, and complete the necessary legal and financial processes. If you plan to rent out the properties, develop effective property management strategies or consider hiring a professional property management company. Regularly monitor and maintain your properties to ensure their long-term profitability.

Monitor and adjust: Continuously monitor the performance of your real estate portfolio and make adjustments as needed.

Stay updated with market trends, rental rates, and property values. Regularly assess the financial viability of each property and consider selling underperforming assets or reinvesting in new opportunities.

Seek professional advice: If you're new to real estate investing or require assistance, consider consulting with 30

professionals such as real estate agents, financial advisors, or property managers. Their expertise can help you make informed decisions and optimize your real estate portfolio.

Remember, creating a real estate portfolio is a long-term endeavor. It requires careful planning, research, and ongoing management. By following these steps and staying informed about the market, you can build a successful real estate investment portfolio.

CHAPTER THREE

Financing Options and Capitalizing on Opportunities
Introduction:

In today's competitive business environment, access to appropriate financing options is crucial for both startups and established companies. It allows businesses to seize growth opportunities, expand operations, and remain competitive.

This note explores various financing options available to businesses and highlights strategies for capitalizing on opportunities.

I. **Financing Options:**

A. **Equity Financing:**

Initial Public Offering (IPO):

The process of offering shares to the public for the first time.

Provides access to substantial capital and raises the company's profile.

Venture Capital (VC) and Angel Investors: Investment from individuals or firms in exchange for equity.

Suitable for startups with high-growth potential.

Private Equity:

Investment in established companies to facilitate expansion or restructuring.

Typically involves substantial investments in return for equity ownership.

B. **Debt Financing:**

Bank Loans:

Traditional loans provided by banks with defined repayment terms.

Suitable for businesses with steady cash flow and collateral.

Lines of Credit:

Pre-approved borrowing limits that businesses can access as needed.

Offers flexibility for short-term financing needs.

Bonds and Debentures:

Issuing debt securities to raise capital from investors.

Typically suitable for larger companies with a proven track record.

33

C. **Alternative Financing:** Crowdfunding:

Raising funds from a large number of individuals via online platforms.

Particularly beneficial for startups and product development.

Peer-to-Peer (P2P) Lending:

Borrowing from individuals or groups without traditional financial intermediaries.

Offers faster approval processes and potentially lower interest rates.

Grants and Subsidies:

Government or private organizations provide funds for specific purposes.

Commonly available for research, development, or socially impactful projects.

II. **Capitalizing on Opportunities:**

A. Market Research and Analysis:

Identify Emerging Trends:

Stay updated with industry trends and customer demands.

34

Capitalize on emerging markets or innovative products/services.

Competitor Analysis:

Evaluate competitors' strategies, strengths, and weaknesses.

Identify gaps and opportunities for differentiation.

B. **Strategic Partnerships:**

Joint Ventures:

Collaborate with other businesses to pursue mutual opportunities.

Pool resources, expertise, and market reach.

Licensing and Franchising:

License intellectual property or franchise business models to expand quickly.

Leverage the brand and expertise of established partners.

C. **Diversification:**

Product or Service Expansion:

Introduce new products or services to existing or new markets.

Leverage existing customer base and distribution channels.

35

Geographic Expansion:

Expand operations into new geographic regions.

Tap into untapped markets and diversify risk.

D. **Technology Adoption:**

Automation and Efficiency:

Embrace technology to streamline operations and reduce costs.

Free up resources for growth initiatives.

Digital Marketing and E-commerce:

Leverage online platforms to reach a wider audience.

Capitalize on the growing trend of online purchasing.

E. **Talent Acquisition and Development:** Attracting and Retaining Skilled Workforce: Invest in recruitment, training, and development programs.

Foster a culture of innovation and continuous learning.

Collaboration with Educational Institutions: Establish partnerships with universities or training institutions.

36

Access fresh talent and contribute to skill development.

MORTGAGE & LOAN OPTIONS

When it comes to mortgage and loan options, there are several types available depending on your specific needs and circumstances. *Here are some common options:* Conventional Mortgage: This is a traditional mortgage loan offered by banks or lending institutions. It usually requires a down payment, and the interest rate may vary depending on your creditworthiness.

Fixed-Rate Mortgage: With a fixed-rate mortgage, the interest rate remains the same throughout the loan term. This provides stability as your monthly payments will not change, regardless of fluctuations in the market.

Adjustable-Rate Mortgage (ARM): An ARM has an interest rate that adjusts periodically. Typically, there is an initial fixed-rate period (e.g., 3, 5, 7 years), after which the rate can change annually based on market conditions. This option is suitable if you plan to sell or refinance before the rate adjustment period.

37

Federal Housing Administration (FHA) Loan: FHA loans are backed by the Federal Housing Administration and are designed to help first-time homebuyers or those with lower credit scores. They require a lower down payment and have more flexible qualification criteria.

Veterans Affairs (VA) Loan: VA loans are available to eligible veterans, active-duty service members, and surviving spouses. They offer favorable terms, including no down payment and competitive interest rates.

Jumbo Loan: Jumbo loans exceed the loan limits set by government-sponsored enterprises like Fannie Mae and Freddie Mac. They are suitable for financing higher-priced properties but often require a higher credit score, a larger down payment, and more stringent eligibility criteria.

Home Equity Loan: If you own a home, you can borrow against its equity using a home equity loan. The loan amount is based on the difference between your home's value and the outstanding mortgage balance. These loans typically have fixed interest rates and are used for specific purposes.

38

Home Equity Line of Credit (HELOC): A HELOC also uses your home's equity but provides a revolving line of credit, similar to a credit card. You can borrow as needed up to a certain limit and repay it over time. The interest rate may be variable, and the funds can be used for various purposes.

It's important to research and compare the terms, interest rates, fees, and requirements of different mortgage and loan options. Additionally, consult with lenders or mortgage professionals who can provide personalized advice based on your financial situation and goals.

CREATIVE FINANCING TECHNIQUES

Creative financing techniques refer to alternative methods of funding or structuring financial transactions that go beyond traditional approaches. These techniques are often employed in situations where conventional financing options may be limited or when unique circumstances require innovative solutions.

Here are five examples of creative financing techniques: Seller Financing: In this arrangement, the seller of a property or asset provides financing directly to the buyer. Instead of 39

obtaining a loan from a bank, the buyer makes payments to the seller over an agreed-upon period. Seller financing can be beneficial for buyers who may have difficulty qualifying for a traditional mortgage or securing other types of funding.

Venture Capital and Angel Investors: Startups and early-stage companies often turn to venture capitalists (VCs) or angel investors for funding. These individuals or firms provide capital in exchange for equity or ownership stakes in the company. Venture capital and angel investors can offer not only financial resources but also expertise, mentorship, and industry connections.

Crowdfunding: Crowdfunding platforms allow individuals or businesses to raise funds from a large number of people, typically via the internet. Through donations, rewards-based contributions, or investment-style crowdfunding, creators and entrepreneurs can secure funding for various projects or business ventures. Crowdfunding can provide access to capital while also building a supportive community around the project.

Lease-to-Own: Also known as a rent-to-own arrangement, this method allows individuals or businesses to lease a property or asset with an option to purchase it at a later date.

40

A portion of the rent paid during the lease period is often applied toward the purchase price. Lease-to-own agreements can be beneficial for individuals who may not qualify for a mortgage initially but aim to transition into ownership over time.

Factoring: Factoring involves selling accounts receivable or invoices to a third party, known as a factor, at a discount. The factor provides immediate cash flow to the business by advancing a percentage of the invoice value, typically around 80% to 90%. Once the customer pays the invoice, the factor deducts their fee and forwards the remaining balance to the business. Factoring can be useful for businesses that need immediate funds but cannot afford to wait for their customers' payment terms.

It's important to note that while creative financing techniques can offer alternative funding solutions, they may also have specific risks or considerations. It's advisable to seek professional advice and thoroughly evaluate the terms and implications before entering into any creative financing arrangement.

41

Identifying Lucrative Investment Opportunities Identifying lucrative investment opportunities requires a combination of research, analysis, and understanding of various factors that can impact the performance of different asset classes. While I can provide some general guidance, please note that investment decisions should be based on thorough research and consultation with financial professionals.

Here are some steps you can take to identify potential investment opportunities:

Set your investment goals: Determine your investment objectives, such as capital appreciation, income generation, or wealth preservation. This will help you narrow down the types of investments that align with your goals.

Understand your risk tolerance: Assess your risk tolerance level, as it will influence the types of investments you should consider. Generally, higher-risk investments have the potential for higher returns, but also come with increased volatility and the possibility of losses.

Research different asset classes: Explore various asset classes, such as stocks, bonds, real estate, commodities, and 42

cryptocurrencies. Understand their historical performance, risk profiles, and potential returns. Consider diversifying your portfolio by investing in a mix of asset classes to spread risk.

Stay updated with market trends: Follow financial news, economic indicators, and market trends. Look for sectors or industries that are experiencing growth or disruption.

Emerging technologies, demographic shifts, and global events can create investment opportunities.

Fundamental analysis: When evaluating individual stocks, analyze the financial health, competitive position, and growth prospects of the companies. Look at financial statements, earnings reports, management team, and industry dynamics to assess the potential for future success.

Technical analysis: Use technical analysis tools and charts to identify patterns, trends, and support/resistance levels in the price movements of securities. Technical analysis can help you make decisions based on market sentiment and trading patterns.

Seek professional advice: Consider consulting with financial advisors, wealth managers, or investment professionals who 43

can provide personalized guidance based on your financial situation, goals, and risk tolerance. They can offer insights and expertise that may help you identify lucrative investment opportunities.

Evaluate risk-reward ratios: Assess the potential risks and rewards of each investment opportunity. Consider factors such as the potential for capital appreciation, income generation, liquidity, and associated costs (e.g., fees, taxes).

Compare these factors against your investment goals and risk tolerance to determine if the opportunity is suitable.

Diversify your portfolio: Spreading your investments across different asset classes, industries, and geographical regions can help mitigate risk. Diversification can provide stability and potentially increase the chances of capturing profitable opportunities.

Monitor and review: Continuously monitor your investments and review their performance. Stay informed about any changes in the market or specific investments. Regularly assess whether your investments are aligned with your goals and make adjustments as necessary.

44

Remember that investing involves risks, and past performance is not indicative of future results. It's crucial to conduct thorough research and make informed decisions based on your individual circumstances and risk tolerance.

Examples of lucrative investment opportunities While I can provide you with some examples of historically lucrative investment opportunities, it's important to note that past performance is not indicative of future results. The investment landscape is constantly changing, and it's crucial to conduct thorough research and seek advice from financial professionals before making any investment decisions. That being said, here are a few examples of investment opportunities that have shown potential for significant returns in the past:

Stocks: Investing in individual stocks of well-established companies with a track record of growth and profitability can yield lucrative returns. For instance, technology giants like Amazon, Apple, and Google have experienced substantial stock price appreciation over the years.

45

Real Estate: Investing in real estate properties, such as residential homes, commercial buildings, or rental properties, can be profitable over the long term. Real estate investments can generate income through rental payments or appreciation in property value.

Cryptocurrencies: While highly volatile and risky, cryptocurrencies like Bitcoin and Ethereum have delivered substantial returns for some investors. However, it's important to approach crypto investments with caution and only invest what you can afford to lose.

Venture Capital: Investing in early-stage startups with high growth potential can be lucrative if you have an appetite for risk. Successful ventures can provide substantial returns, but it's important to diversify your portfolio due to the high failure rate of startups.

Index Funds: Investing in low-cost index funds that track the performance of broad market indices, such as the S&P 500, can be a relatively safe and lucrative long-term investment strategy. This approach allows you to diversify your investments across a wide range of companies.

46

Renewable Energy: As the world shifts towards clean energy, investing in renewable energy companies or projects can be a lucrative opportunity. This sector has experienced significant growth in recent years, driven by increased demand and government initiatives.

Remember, each investment opportunity comes with its own risks and rewards. It's essential to conduct thorough research, assess your risk tolerance, and consider your investment goals before committing your capital to any investment opportunity.

47

CHAPTER FOUR

PROPERTY SELECTION AND DUE DILIGENCE

Introduction:

Property selection and due diligence are critical processes in real estate investment. Whether you're an individual looking to buy a home or a seasoned investor interested in commercial properties, conducting thorough due diligence is essential to mitigate risks and make informed decisions.

This guide aims to provide a comprehensive overview of property selection and due diligence, covering key steps and considerations involved in the process.

I. **Property Selection:**

Define your investment goals: Start by clearly outlining your investment objectives. Determine whether you're looking for long-term appreciation, rental income, or a combination of both. This will help you focus on properties that align with your goals.

Research the market: Study the local real estate market to understand trends, supply and demand dynamics, and potential growth areas. Look for factors such as job growth, 48

infrastructure development, and proximity to amenities, as these can influence property values.

Identify property types: Based on your investment goals, determine the type of property that suits your needs. Options include residential properties (single-family homes, condos, apartments), commercial properties (office buildings, retail spaces), or specialized properties (industrial, healthcare, etc.).

Set a budget: Establish a realistic budget based on your financial capacity and investment goals. Consider not only the property purchase price but also additional costs like maintenance, taxes, insurance, and potential renovations.

Define property criteria: Create a list of desirable property characteristics such as location, size, amenities, and potential for future appreciation. Prioritize these criteria to streamline your search process and focus on properties that meet your requirements.

II. **Due Diligence:**

Engage professionals: Assemble a team of professionals including real estate agents, lawyers, accountants, and 49

property inspectors to assist with the due diligence process.

Their expertise can help identify potential issues and provide valuable insights.

Review legal aspects: Examine legal documents related to the property, including title deeds, surveys, zoning regulations, and any existing liens or encumbrances. Verify the property's legal compliance and ensure there are no legal disputes or pending litigation.

Conduct property inspections: Hire a qualified property inspector to thoroughly assess the physical condition of the property. Inspections should cover structural integrity, electrical and plumbing systems, HVAC, and any other relevant components. Address any major issues that may affect the property's value or require significant repairs.

Evaluate financials: Scrutinize financial documents such as income and expense statements, rent rolls, and utility bills for commercial properties. For residential properties, analyze rental income potential and compare it with market rates.

Assess the property's financial viability and potential return on investment.

50

Assess market value: Obtain a professional appraisal to determine the fair market value of the property. Appraisals provide an objective evaluation based on comparable sales, property condition, location, and market factors. Compare the appraised value with the asking price to negotiate effectively.

Investigate zoning and permits: Research local zoning regulations to ensure the property is designated for its intended use. Check for any pending or expired permits and understand any potential restrictions or limitations that could impact your investment plans.

Analyze environmental factors: Assess the property for environmental risks, such as contamination or proximity to environmentally sensitive areas. Conduct environmental assessments or consult with experts to identify any potential liabilities and evaluate the associated costs.

Review lease agreements (for commercial properties): If acquiring a property with existing tenants, carefully review lease agreements to understand lease terms, rent payment history, and any pending lease renewals or terminations.

Evaluate the tenant's financial stability and their impact on the property's cash flow.

51

Conclusion:

Property selection and due diligence are fundamental steps in real estate investment. Thoroughly researching the market, defining investment

EVALUATING PROPERTY VALUE

Introduction:

Evaluating the value of a property is a crucial step in various real estate transactions. Whether you are buying, selling, refinancing, or investing in property, understanding its value is essential.

This note provides an overview of the key factors and approaches involved in evaluating property value.

I. **Market Analysis:**

Local Market Research:

Gather information about the local real estate market, including recent sales, current listings, and trends.

Consider factors such as location, neighborhood amenities, schools, transportation, and future development plans.

52

Comparable Sales:

Identify recently sold properties that are similar in location, size, condition, and features to the property being evaluated.

Analyze the sale prices of comparable properties to estimate the value of the subject property.

II. **Property-Specific Factors:**

Physical Characteristics:

Assess the property's size, including land area and square footage of buildings.

Consider the number of bedrooms, bathrooms, and other amenities.

Evaluate the condition of the property, including any upgrades or renovations.

Location:

Examine the proximity to amenities like schools, parks, shopping centers, and transportation hubs.

Evaluate the desirability of the neighborhood, including safety, cleanliness, and community appeal.

Consider any geographic factors that may impact value, such as views, waterfront access, or natural hazards.

53

Property Condition:

Inspect the property for any structural issues, damages, or maintenance requirements.

Consider the age of the property and the condition of its systems (electrical, plumbing, HVAC, etc.).

Take note of any necessary repairs or renovations and their potential impact on value.

III. Appraisal Methods:

Sales Comparison Approach:

Focuses on recent comparable sales to estimate the property's value.

Adjust the sale prices of comparable properties to account for differences in size, condition, features, and market conditions.

Calculate an estimated value based on the adjusted sales prices.

Cost Approach:

Estimates the value based on the cost of replacing the property.

Assess the land value and estimate the cost to construct a similar property.

Consider depreciation and obsolescence factors.

54

Income Approach:

Applicable for income-generating properties (e.g., rental properties, commercial buildings).

Estimate the property's value based on its income potential and the prevailing capitalization rate.

Analyze rental income, operating expenses, vacancy rates, and market rental rates.

IV. **Professional Assistance:**

Real Estate Agents:

Engage with experienced local real estate agents who have in-depth knowledge of the market and can provide comparative market analyses.

Seek their guidance on pricing strategies and property valuation.

Appraisers:

Hire professional appraisers qualified to evaluate property value accurately.

Appraisers follow standardized methods and consider various factors to provide an unbiased opinion of value.

Conclusion:

55

Evaluating property value involves a comprehensive analysis of market trends, property-specific factors, and the application of appropriate appraisal methods. By considering these factors and seeking professional assistance when needed, individuals can make informed decisions regarding property transactions, investments, or financing. Remember that property values can fluctuate over time, so regular evaluations are recommended to stay updated with market conditions.

CONDUCTING MARKET RESEARCH

Introduction:

Market research is a crucial process that helps businesses gather information and insights about their target market, customers, competitors, and industry trends. It enables businesses to make informed decisions, develop effective strategies, and stay competitive in the marketplace.

This note provides an overview of the key steps involved in conducting market research.

Define the Research Objective:

56

Before starting any market research initiative, it is essential to clearly define the research objective. Determine what specific information you aim to obtain and how it will support your business goals. For example, you might want to understand customer preferences, evaluate market demand for a new product, or assess the effectiveness of your marketing campaigns.

Identify the Target Market:

Identifying the target market is crucial for conducting effective market research. Define the characteristics and demographics of your target audience, such as age, gender, location, income level, and purchasing behavior. This helps ensure that the research findings are relevant and applicable to your business.

Choose the Research Methodology:

There are various research methodologies available, including primary research and secondary research.

a. Primary Research:

Primary research involves collecting data directly from the target market. Common primary research methods include surveys, interviews, focus groups, and observations. Surveys can be conducted online, via telephone, or in person.

57

Interviews can be conducted one-on-one or in a group setting. Focus groups bring together a small group of individuals to discuss specific topics. Observations involve watching and recording consumer behavior.

b. Secondary Research:

Secondary research involves analyzing existing data and information that has been previously collected by other sources. This includes industry reports, government publications, academic studies, and market research reports.

Secondary research provides valuable insights and can help validate primary research findings.

Develop a Research Plan:

Create a detailed research plan outlining the specific activities, timeline, and resources required for your market research. This plan should include the research objectives, target market description, chosen research methodology, sample size determination, data collection tools, and analysis techniques.

Collect Data:

Implement the research plan by collecting data according to the chosen research methodology. If conducting primary research, administer surveys, conduct interviews or focus 58

groups, or observe consumer behavior. Ensure that the data collection process is consistent, unbiased, and accurate.

Analyze Data:

Once the data is collected, it needs to be analyzed to derive meaningful insights. Use statistical tools, data analysis software, or qualitative analysis techniques to interpret the data. Identify patterns, trends, correlations, and outliers that can help answer the research questions and support decision-making.

Interpret and Draw Conclusions:

Based on the analysis, interpret the findings and draw conclusions. Determine what the data reveals about customer preferences, market trends, competitor strategies, or any other research objectives. Relate the findings back to your business goals and evaluate how they can inform your marketing, product development, or business strategies.

Report and Present Findings:

Present the market research findings in a clear and concise report. Include an executive summary, research methodology, key findings, analysis, conclusions, and recommendations.

Use charts, graphs, and visuals to enhance understanding. If 59

necessary, present the findings to stakeholders, management, or relevant teams within your organization.

Take Action:

Market research is most valuable when it leads to action.

Utilize the insights gained to make informed business decisions. Implement changes to marketing strategies, product offerings, pricing, or customer targeting based on the research findings. Regularly review and update your market research efforts to stay current with changing market dynamics.

Conclusion:

Conducting market research is a vital process for businesses seeking to understand their target market, customers, and industry landscape.

Assessing Property Condition and Potential Property condition and potential assessment is an important process that helps individuals or organizations evaluate the condition of a property, identify any potential issues or 60

opportunities, and make informed decisions regarding its purchase, renovation, or ongoing maintenance.

This note provides an overview of the key factors to consider when assessing property condition and potential.

Physical Inspection:

Perform a thorough physical inspection of the property to assess its overall condition. This includes examining the structure, foundation, roof, walls, windows, doors, plumbing, electrical systems, HVAC (heating, ventilation, and air conditioning) systems, and any other relevant components.

Look for signs of damage, deterioration, or potential hazards.

Structural Integrity:

Assess the structural integrity of the property to determine if there are any major structural issues that could affect its stability and safety. Look for cracks in the walls or foundation, uneven floors, or sagging ceilings. Consider hiring a professional structural engineer to conduct a detailed evaluation if necessary.

Building Code Compliance:

Check if the property complies with local building codes and regulations. Non-compliance can lead to legal and financial 61

consequences. Identify any code violations and determine the cost and effort required to rectify them.

Maintenance History:

Review the maintenance history of the property to understand how well it has been maintained over time. This includes evaluating records of repairs, renovations, and routine maintenance tasks. A well-maintained property is likely to have fewer issues and may indicate responsible ownership.

Environmental Factors:

Consider environmental factors that could impact the property's condition and potential. This includes assessing the risk of natural disasters such as flooding, earthquakes, or hurricanes. Additionally, check for the presence of hazardous materials like asbestos, lead paint, or mold, which may require remediation or abatement.

Location and Neighborhood:

Evaluate the property's location and the surrounding neighborhood. Factors such as proximity to amenities, schools, public transportation, and crime rates can affect the property's desirability and potential for appreciation.

62

Research future development plans or zoning changes that could impact the property value.

Market Analysis:

Conduct a market analysis to assess the property's potential value and demand. Evaluate recent comparable sales in the area to determine its market value. Consider future market trends and potential growth opportunities that could impact the property's value over time.

Potential for Improvement:

Identify the potential for improvement or expansion of the property. Evaluate factors such as available space for additions, remodeling possibilities, or zoning regulations that may affect future development plans. Consider the cost and feasibility of such improvements and estimate the potential return on investment.

Legal and Financial Considerations:

Review any legal or financial aspects associated with the property. This includes examining property titles, liens, easements, and any outstanding mortgages or debts. Engage with professionals such as real estate attorneys and financial advisors to ensure a clear understanding of the property's legal and financial implications.

63

Professional Assistance: Seek professional assistance from qualified experts such as home inspectors, structural engineers, real estate agents, and appraisers. Their expertise can provide valuable insights and help in making informed decisions about the property's condition and potential.

Remember, assessing property condition and potential requires a comprehensive and systematic approach. By considering the factors mentioned above and seeking professional guidance, you can make well-informed decisions regarding property acquisition, renovation, or ongoing maintenance.

64

CHAPTER FIVE

NEGOTIATION AND ACQUISITION STRATEGIES

Introduction:

Negotiation and acquisition strategies are crucial elements in business and organizational environments. These strategies involve the process of reaching mutually beneficial agreements, acquiring assets or companies, and ensuring long-term success in various business dealings.

This comprehensive note will provide an overview of negotiation and acquisition strategies, discussing key concepts, techniques, and best practices.

I. Negotiation Strategies:

A. Preparation:

Define objectives: Clearly articulate the desired outcomes and goals of the negotiation.

Gather information: Conduct thorough research on the other party, their interests, and potential alternatives.

Assess strengths and weaknesses: Identify your own strengths and weaknesses, as well as those of the other party.

65

Determine negotiation tactics: Select appropriate negotiation tactics based on the context and desired outcomes.

B. Building Relationships:

Establish rapport: Build trust and rapport with the other party through effective communication and active listening.

Focus on mutual interests: Seek common ground and identify shared interests to foster collaboration.

Manage emotions: Keep emotions in check and maintain a professional demeanor throughout the negotiation process.

Practice empathy: Understand the perspectives and concerns of the other party to find mutually agreeable solutions.

C. Communication and Persuasion:

Active listening: Listen actively to the other party's concerns, needs, and preferences.

Effective communication: Clearly articulate your own position, expectations, and offers.

Persuasion techniques: Utilize persuasive strategies such as logical reasoning, storytelling, and providing evidence.

Problem-solving approach: Adopt a collaborative problem-solving mindset to find win-win solutions.

D. Concessions and Compromises:

66

Prioritize interests: Focus on underlying interests rather than rigid positions.

Make calculated concessions: Offer concessions strategically, ensuring that they align with your overall objectives.

Seek reciprocity: Encourage the other party to reciprocate concessions to maintain balance in the negotiation process.

Creative solutions: Explore alternative options and propose innovative solutions to bridge gaps and facilitate agreement.

II. Acquisition Strategies:

A. Strategic Planning:

Define acquisition objectives: Clearly articulate the purpose and strategic goals of the acquisition.

Conduct due diligence: Thoroughly evaluate the target company's financials, operations, legal status, and potential risks.

Assess compatibility: Evaluate the compatibility of the target company's culture, values, and long-term vision with your own organization.

Establish integration plans: Develop a comprehensive plan to integrate the acquired company into your existing operations smoothly.

B. Valuation and Negotiation:

67

Determine valuation methods: Utilize various valuation techniques, such as discounted cash flow analysis or market comparables, to establish a fair acquisition price.

Negotiate deal terms: Engage in negotiations with the target company to agree on purchase price, payment terms, and other relevant terms and conditions.

Non-disclosure agreements: Implement confidentiality agreements to protect sensitive information during the negotiation phase.

Seek legal and financial advice: Consult legal and financial professionals to ensure compliance with laws and regulations and to obtain expert guidance throughout the acquisition process.

C. Risk Management:

Identify potential risks: Conduct a thorough risk assessment to identify potential pitfalls and challenges associated with the acquisition.

Mitigate risks: Develop risk mitigation strategies to address identified risks and minimize their impact.

Develop contingency plans: Prepare contingency plans to handle unexpected circumstances that may arise during or after the acquisition.

Communication and stakeholder management: Maintain open and transparent communication with stakeholders, 68

including employees, customers, and investors, to manage their expectations and address concerns.

Post-Acquisition Integration:

Cultural integration: Foster integration of employees and align cultures, values, and operating practices to ensure a smooth transition. Recognize and respect the cultural differences between the acquiring and acquired organizations. Encourage open communication and collaboration to bridge any gaps and build a cohesive company culture.

Synergy realization: Identify areas of synergy between the acquiring and acquired organizations and develop plans to capitalize on them. This may include streamlining processes, leveraging shared resources, and eliminating redundancies.

Set clear goals and timelines for achieving synergies and monitor progress regularly.

Organizational restructuring: Assess the organizational structure and make necessary adjustments to optimize efficiency and effectiveness. This may involve reassigning roles and responsibilities, integrating teams, or creating new reporting lines. Communicate any changes transparently to minimize uncertainty and resistance.

69

Integration of systems and operations: Evaluate the existing systems, processes, and technologies of both organizations and integrate them where appropriate. This may involve implementing new software, aligning IT infrastructure, or standardizing operational procedures. Ensure proper training and support are provided to employees to adapt to any changes.

Talent retention and development: Develop strategies to retain key talent from the acquired organization. Provide opportunities for professional growth and development, and offer incentives to retain top performers. Foster a supportive and inclusive environment that values the contributions of all employees.

Customer and supplier management: Maintain open lines of communication with customers and suppliers of both organizations to ensure a seamless transition. Address any concerns or issues promptly and proactively. Develop strategies to leverage the combined customer base and supplier network for mutual benefit.

Financial integration: Consolidate financial systems and reporting to gain a comprehensive view of the combined 70

organization's financial performance. Streamline financial processes, including budgeting, forecasting, and reporting, to improve efficiency and accuracy. Ensure compliance with financial regulations and standards.

Change management and communication: Implement a robust change management plan to guide employees through the integration process. Communicate the vision, goals, and progress of the integration regularly and transparently.

Address employee concerns and provide support to alleviate any anxiety or resistance to change.

Performance monitoring and evaluation: Establish key performance indicators (KPIs) to assess the success of the integration efforts. Continuously monitor and evaluate the progress against set targets. Make necessary adjustments as needed to ensure the integration is on track and delivering the desired outcomes.

Continuous improvement: Foster a culture of continuous improvement throughout the integration process. Encourage feedback from employees at all levels and implement suggestions for enhancing integration efforts. Learn from challenges and successes to refine future acquisition and integration strategies.

71

By effectively managing the post-acquisition integration process, organizations can maximize the value of the acquisition, realize synergies, and position themselves for long-term success.

EFFECTIVE NEGOTIATION TECHNIQUES

Introduction:

Negotiation is a crucial skill that plays a significant role in various aspects of life, including business, relationships, and conflict resolution. Mastering effective negotiation techniques can greatly enhance your ability to achieve favorable outcomes and maintain positive relationships.

This note will outline several key techniques that can help you become a more skilled negotiator.

Preparation:

One of the fundamental pillars of effective negotiation is thorough preparation. Before entering a negotiation, it is essential to research and gather relevant information about the subject matter, the other party involved, and any potential alternatives or options. This preparation allows you to have a 72

clear understanding of your own objectives, as well as the strengths and weaknesses of both parties, providing a solid foundation for the negotiation process.

Active Listening:

Active listening is a critical skill in negotiation. It involves not only hearing the words spoken by the other party but also paying attention to their tone, body language, and underlying interests. By actively listening, you can demonstrate empathy and understanding, which can help build rapport and create a more cooperative atmosphere. Additionally, it allows you to gather valuable information that can be used to find common ground and generate mutually beneficial solutions.

Effective Communication:

Clear and concise communication is vital during a negotiation. Express your ideas, needs, and concerns in a respectful and assertive manner. Be mindful of your tone and body language, ensuring that they convey confidence and respect. Clearly articulate your expectations and desired outcomes, and encourage the other party to do the same.

Open and honest communication helps establish trust and enables both parties to work towards finding mutually satisfactory agreements.

73

Establishing Common Ground: Finding common ground is essential for successful negotiations. Look for shared interests or goals that can form the basis of an agreement. By focusing on areas of agreement, you can build momentum and create a sense of collaboration. Identifying common ground can also help overcome potential conflicts and allow both parties to explore creative solutions that meet their needs.

Win-Win Mindset:

A win-win mindset involves seeking outcomes that benefit both parties involved in the negotiation. Avoid adopting a win-lose mentality, where one party gains at the expense of the other. Instead, strive to find solutions that satisfy the interests of both parties. This approach promotes long-term relationships, encourages cooperation, and enhances the likelihood of future successful negotiations.

Flexibility and Adaptability:

Negotiations rarely proceed according to a predetermined script. It is crucial to remain flexible and adaptable throughout the process. Be open to exploring alternative options and be willing to adjust your position based on new information or changing circumstances. Embracing flexibility allows you to respond effectively to unforeseen 74 challenges and increases the chances of reaching a mutually beneficial agreement.

Problem Solving:

Approach negotiations as an opportunity to solve problems rather than engage in a battle. By framing the negotiation as a joint effort to address and overcome challenges, both parties can focus on finding creative solutions. This problem-solving mindset encourages collaboration, generates innovative ideas, and fosters a more productive negotiation environment.

Patience and Persistence:

Negotiations can be complex and time-consuming. It is important to exercise patience and persistence throughout the process. Avoid rushing into agreements or succumbing to pressure. Take the necessary time to fully explore options and consider various perspectives. Be persistent in pursuing mutually beneficial outcomes, even when faced with obstacles or setbacks. Patience and persistence can lead to more favorable results and strengthen the negotiation process.

Conclusion:

75

Effective negotiation techniques are essential skills for achieving successful outcomes in various personal and professional scenarios. By preparing thoroughly, actively listening, communicating effectively, establishing common ground, adopting a win-win mindset, being flexible, embracing problem-solving, and demonstrating patience and persistence, you can significantly improve your negotiation abilities. Remember that negotiation is a dynamic process, **MAKING SUCCESSFUL OFFERS**

Introduction:

In the world of business and negotiations, making successful offers is a crucial skill. Whether you are a salesperson, entrepreneur, or professional looking to strike a deal, understanding the key elements of a successful offer is essential.

This note will outline the important factors to consider when making offers, from understanding your target audience to crafting compelling proposals that increase the likelihood of acceptance.

Research and Understand Your Target Audience: 76

Before making an offer, it is essential to research and understand your target audience. This includes identifying their needs, preferences, and pain points. By gaining a deep understanding of their motivations and goals, you can tailor your offer to resonate with their specific desires and challenges. This research will enable you to position your offer effectively and increase its chances of success.

Clearly Define the Value Proposition:

The value proposition is a crucial component of a successful offer. Clearly articulate the unique value your product, service, or proposal brings to the table. Highlight the benefits, advantages, and solutions it offers to the target audience. Emphasize how your offer can address their pain points, save them time or money, or provide them with a competitive advantage. A compelling value proposition is more likely to grab the attention and interest of potential buyers.

Competitive Analysis:

Conduct a thorough competitive analysis to identify your strengths and weaknesses compared to similar offerings in the market. Highlight the aspects that differentiate your offer and make it superior. By understanding the competitive landscape, you can address any objections or concerns that 77

may arise and position your offer as the best choice among alternatives.

Personalize and Customize:

Tailor your offer to each individual or organization you are presenting it to. Generic offers may appear impersonal and fail to capture the attention of the recipient. Personalization demonstrates that you have taken the time to understand their specific needs and have crafted a proposal that aligns with their objectives. Customize your offer by highlighting how it addresses their unique challenges and provides value in a way that is relevant to them.

Communicate Clearly and Compellingly:

When presenting your offer, ensure that your communication is clear, concise, and compelling. Use language that is easy to understand, avoiding technical jargon or complex terms that may confuse your audience. Structure your offer in a logical manner, emphasizing the most important points first.

Utilize visual aids, such as charts or infographics, to enhance clarity and engage your audience. Clearly outline the terms, conditions, and pricing of your offer to avoid any misunderstandings.

Provide Social Proof and Testimonials: 78

Incorporate social proof and testimonials into your offer to build credibility and trust. Share success stories, case studies, or testimonials from satisfied customers who have benefited from your product or service. This evidence demonstrates that your offer has a track record of delivering results, increasing the likelihood of acceptance.

Follow-Up and Address Concerns:

After presenting your offer, follow up with the recipient to address any concerns or questions they may have. Be responsive and proactive in providing additional information or clarification. This shows your commitment to their satisfaction and can help overcome any remaining objections they may have.

Conclusion:

Making successful offers requires a strategic approach that combines thorough research, a compelling value proposition, customization, clear communication, and addressing concerns. By understanding your target audience, crafting personalized offers, and effectively conveying the value of your proposition, you can significantly increase the chances of your offers being accepted and achieving successful outcomes in negotiations and business transactions.

79

CLOSING THE DEAL

Introduction:

Closing the deal is a critical stage in any business transaction. It refers to the finalization and agreement between parties involved, where a mutually beneficial arrangement is reached. This process requires effective communication, negotiation skills, and understanding of the needs and expectations of all parties.

In this comprehensive guide, we will outline key strategies and techniques to help you successfully close a deal.

Establish Rapport and Trust:

Building rapport and trust with the other party is essential for a successful deal closure. Take the time to establish a positive relationship, understand their needs, and demonstrate credibility and expertise. Active listening and effective communication play a crucial role in gaining their trust.

Understand the Decision-Making Process: Before attempting to close a deal, it is important to understand the decision-making process of the other party.

Identify the key decision-makers involved, their roles, and 80 their decision criteria. This knowledge will help you tailor your approach and address their specific concerns and preferences.

Address Objections and Concerns:

During negotiations, objections and concerns are likely to arise. It is crucial to address these issues promptly and effectively. Listen attentively to the concerns raised, empathize with the other party, and offer viable solutions or alternatives. Demonstrating your commitment to resolving their concerns can significantly enhance your chances of closing the deal.

Highlight Unique Value Proposition:

Clearly communicate the unique value proposition your product, service, or solution offers. Emphasize how it meets the specific needs of the other party and sets you apart from competitors. Showcase success stories, testimonials, or case studies to illustrate the benefits and value they can expect from the deal.

Create a Win-Win Outcome:

Successful deal closures often result in a win-win outcome, where both parties feel satisfied with the agreement. Focus on identifying mutual benefits and ensure that the deal offers 81

advantages for both sides. This approach strengthens the partnership and fosters a positive, long-term relationship.

Use Effective Negotiation Techniques:

Negotiation plays a significant role in closing a deal. Use proven negotiation techniques such as anchoring (setting the initial terms), bundling (offering additional value), and concessions (making reasonable compromises). However, be mindful not to concede too much, as it may undermine the value of your offering.

Summarize and Gain Agreement:

Before closing the deal, summarize the key points and terms of the agreement. Ensure that both parties are aligned on the essential details, including pricing, deliverables, timelines, and any additional conditions. Gain explicit agreement from all decision-makers involved to avoid misunderstandings or disputes later on.

Handle Legal and Documentation Aspects: Once the agreement is reached, handle the necessary legal and documentation aspects promptly. Engage legal experts to draft or review contracts, agreements, and other relevant paperwork. Ensure compliance with legal requirements, 82

protect the interests of both parties, and address any outstanding concerns.

Follow-Up and Maintain Relationships:

Closing the deal does not mark the end of your relationship with the other party. Maintain regular communication, provide post-sale support, and follow up to ensure their satisfaction. Cultivating strong, ongoing relationships can lead to future opportunities, referrals, and potential collaborations.

Conclusion:

Closing the deal is a crucial step in business transactions, requiring effective communication, negotiation skills, and a deep understanding of the needs and expectations of all parties involved. By establishing rapport, addressing concerns, emphasizing value, and utilizing effective negotiation techniques, you can increase your chances of successfully closing a deal. Remember to create a win-win outcome, summarize the agreement, and handle legal aspects meticulously. Maintaining relationships beyond the deal closure ensures long-term success and opportunities for future collaboration.

83

CHAPTER SIX

PROPERTY MANAGEMENT AND MAINTENANCE

Introduction:

Property management and maintenance refer to the processes and activities involved in effectively overseeing and caring for real estate properties. It entails various tasks, including property acquisition, tenant management, maintenance and repairs, financial management, and legal compliance.

This note provides a comprehensive overview of property management and maintenance, highlighting key responsibilities and best practices.

I. Property Management:

Property management encompasses the overall administration and operation of a property. It involves a range of responsibilities to ensure the property is well-maintained and financially sustainable.

Property Acquisition:

Conducting market research and analysis to identify potential properties for investment or management.

Evaluating property value, location, condition, and potential for generating rental income.

84

Negotiating purchase or lease agreements and conducting due diligence.

Tenant Management:

Advertising and marketing vacant units to attract potential tenants.

Screening prospective tenants through background checks, credit checks, and rental history verification.

Preparing and executing lease agreements, including rent collection and security deposits.

Addressing tenant inquiries, complaints, and resolving disputes.

Conducting regular property inspections and enforcing lease terms and regulations.

Maintenance and Repairs:

Implementing regular maintenance schedules to ensure the property's physical condition and functionality.

Conducting preventive maintenance tasks, such as HVAC

servicing, plumbing inspections, and landscaping.

Managing and coordinating repairs and renovations, including obtaining quotes, hiring contractors, and overseeing the work.

Handling emergency maintenance issues promptly to minimize tenant disruptions.

85

Maintaining accurate records of maintenance activities and expenses.

Financial Management:

Establishing and managing the property's budget, including income, expenses, and reserves.

Collecting rent payments, tracking delinquencies, and enforcing late payment penalties.

Paying property-related expenses, such as mortgages, insurance, property taxes, utilities, and maintenance costs.

Conducting regular financial reporting and analysis to monitor profitability and identify areas for improvement.

Setting rental rates based on market trends and property value.

Legal and Regulatory Compliance:

Staying updated on local, state, and federal laws related to property management, rental agreements, and tenant rights.

Ensuring compliance with fair housing laws, building codes, health and safety regulations, and environmental standards.

Managing eviction processes in accordance with legal requirements and due process.

Maintaining proper documentation, including lease agreements, tenant records, and financial transactions.

II. **Property Maintenance:**

86

Property maintenance focuses on preserving the condition and functionality of the property to enhance its longevity and value. It involves regular inspections, repairs, and improvements.

Preventive Maintenance:

Developing a maintenance schedule that includes routine inspections, cleaning, and servicing of essential systems.

Inspecting and maintaining HVAC systems, electrical wiring, plumbing, and roofing.

Conducting regular pest control measures to prevent infestations.

Maintaining common areas, such as hallways, staircases, elevators, and parking lots.

Corrective Maintenance:

Responding promptly to tenant-reported issues, such as plumbing leaks, electrical problems, or appliance malfunctions.

Assessing the severity of maintenance requests and prioritizing them accordingly.

Hiring qualified contractors or technicians to address repairs and replacements.

Documenting repair activities, including invoices, warranties, and completion dates.

87

Cosmetic and Aesthetic Upkeep: Regularly refreshing and updating the property's appearance, both inside and outside.

Painting walls, replacing flooring, and updating fixtures to maintain a modern and appealing look.

Landscaping and gardening to enhance curb appeal.

Cleaning common areas, including lobbies, corridors, and shared facilities.

Capital Improvements:

Planning and implementing major renovations or upgrades to improve the property's value, energy efficiency, or tenant satisfaction.

Examples include roof replacements, HVAC

RENTAL PROPERTY MANAGEMENT

Rental property management involves the operation, maintenance, and oversight of properties that are leased to tenants. It includes various tasks such as advertising vacancies, screening tenants, collecting rent, handling repairs and maintenance, and ensuring compliance with legal and financial obligations.

88

Overview of rental property management: Property Advertising and Marketing:

Identify target rental market and determine competitive rental rates.

Develop a comprehensive marketing strategy to attract potential tenants.

Advertise vacancies through various channels such as online listings, signage, and local publications.

Show the property to interested tenants and provide necessary information.

Tenant Screening and Selection:

Create a tenant screening process to assess applicants'

creditworthiness, rental history, and employment status.

Conduct background and reference checks to verify information provided by applicants.

Select reliable and responsible tenants who meet the established criteria.

Obtain signed lease agreements and collect security deposits.

Rent Collection and Financial Management: Establish clear rent payment policies and communicate them to tenants.

89

Collect rent payments on time and keep accurate records of all transactions.

Handle late payments and initiate eviction processes, if necessary.

Maintain financial records, including income and expense statements, for tax and accounting purposes.

Ensure compliance with local and national financial regulations.

Property Maintenance and Repairs:

Conduct regular inspections of the property to identify maintenance needs.

Coordinate and oversee repairs, renovations, and routine maintenance tasks.

Respond promptly to tenant complaints or repair requests.

Maintain relationships with reliable contractors and service providers.

Keep detailed records of maintenance activities and expenses.

Tenant Relations and Communication:

Establish effective communication channels with tenants.

Address tenant concerns, inquiries, and complaints in a timely and professional manner.

90

Provide necessary information and guidance on lease terms, policies, and procedures.

Foster positive tenant relationships to encourage lease renewals and minimize turnover.

Legal Compliance:

Stay up-to-date with local, state, and federal laws and regulations related to rental properties.

Ensure compliance with fair housing laws and avoid discrimination.

Prepare and enforce lease agreements that protect the rights of both landlords and tenants.

Handle legal procedures such as evictions, lease terminations, and security deposit disputes.

Property Inspections and Documentation: Conduct move-in and move-out inspections to document property condition.

Create detailed inspection reports and photographs to record any damages or repairs needed.

Regularly inspect common areas and perform preventative maintenance tasks.

Maintain organized and accurate records of property-related documentation, including leases, contracts, and correspondence.

91

Insurance and Risk Management: Secure appropriate insurance coverage for the property, such as property insurance and liability insurance.

Identify and mitigate potential risks and hazards on the property.

Implement safety measures and ensure compliance with building codes and regulations.

Handle insurance claims and communicate with insurance providers, if necessary.

Financial Reporting and Analysis:

Prepare regular financial reports that outline income, expenses, and profitability of the rental property.

Analyze financial data to identify trends, opportunities for cost reduction, and areas for improvement.

Monitor market conditions and adjust rental rates accordingly.

Develop and manage property budgets.

Continuous Education and Professional Development: Stay informed about industry trends, best practices, and new regulations.

Attend workshops, seminars, and conferences related to property management.

92

Join professional associations or networks to connect with other property managers and share insights.

Effective rental property management requires attention to detail, strong organizational and communication skills, and a good understanding of legal and financial aspects. By efficiently managing rental properties, property owners can maximize returns on their

PROPERTY MAINTENANCE AND UPKEEP

Property maintenance and upkeep refer to the activities and tasks involved in preserving, repairing, and ensuring the proper functioning and appearance of a property. Whether it is a residential, commercial, or industrial property, regular maintenance is crucial for its longevity, value, and overall functionality.

This note provides an overview of property maintenance and upkeep, including its importance, key areas of focus, and best practices.

Importance of Property Maintenance and Upkeep:
Preservation of Property Value: Regular maintenance helps maintain the property's value and prevents depreciation over 93

time. Well-maintained properties are more appealing to potential buyers or tenants and can command higher prices or rents.

Safety and Security: Proper upkeep ensures the safety and security of occupants and visitors. Regular inspections and maintenance can identify potential hazards, such as faulty wiring, structural weaknesses, or fire hazards, and address them promptly.

Cost Savings: Timely maintenance and repairs can prevent minor issues from escalating into major problems, saving significant costs in the long run. Proactive maintenance helps avoid expensive emergency repairs and extends the lifespan of building systems and components.

Compliance with Regulations: Property owners have legal obligations to meet certain maintenance standards and adhere to building codes and regulations. Regular upkeep helps ensure compliance, avoiding potential legal issues and penalties.

Tenant Satisfaction: For rental properties, well-maintained premises contribute to tenant satisfaction and retention. A comfortable and well-functioning property enhances the 94

tenant's experience, fostering a positive relationship with the property owner or management.

Key Areas of Property Maintenance and Upkeep: Exterior Maintenance: This includes tasks related to the building's exterior, such as roof inspections, gutter cleaning, façade repairs, painting, landscaping, and parking lot maintenance.

Interior Maintenance: Focuses on maintaining the interior spaces, including plumbing, electrical systems, HVAC (heating, ventilation, and air conditioning), flooring, walls, ceilings, and fixtures. Regular inspections, filter replacements, and repairs are essential.

Structural Maintenance. Involves monitoring and addressing issues related to the building's structure, foundation, walls, and supports. Structural inspections can identify signs of damage, such as cracks, settlement, or dampness, which require immediate attention.

Systems and Equipment Maintenance: Refers to the upkeep of various systems and equipment within the property, including heating and cooling systems, plumbing fixtures, 95

electrical panels, elevators, security systems, and fire safety equipment. Regular servicing, testing, and preventive maintenance are vital.

Regular Cleaning: Maintaining a clean and hygienic environment is crucial for both the appearance and health of the property. Regular cleaning includes tasks such as dusting, vacuuming, mopping, window cleaning, and waste management.

Best Practices for Property Maintenance and Upkeep:
Establish a Maintenance Schedule: Develop a comprehensive maintenance schedule that outlines routine tasks, inspections, and maintenance activities. This helps ensure that maintenance is performed regularly and systematically.

Conduct Regular Inspections: Regularly inspect the property to identify any maintenance issues or potential problems.

Create checklists to ensure thorough inspections and address issues promptly.

Prioritize Repairs: Assess the urgency and severity of maintenance issues and prioritize repairs accordingly.

Critical safety or structural issues should be addressed 96

immediately, while minor cosmetic repairs can be scheduled at a later date.

Engage Professional Service Providers: For complex repairs or specialized tasks, it is advisable to engage professional service providers with expertise in the relevant areas. This includes contractors, electricians, plumbers, landscapers, and HVAC technicians.

Maintain Documentation: Keep detailed records of all maintenance and repair activities, including dates, descriptions, and costs. Documentation helps track the property's maintenance history, warranty information, and compliance with regulations.

Communicate with Occupants

Effective communication is crucial for maintaining positive relationships with occupants and ensuring the smooth operation of properties. Here are some tips: Be clear and concise: When communicating with occupants, use simple and easy-to-understand language. Avoid jargon or technical terms that may confuse them. Clearly convey your message and provide relevant details.

97

Use various communication channels: Use a mix of communication channels to reach occupants effectively. This may include email, phone calls, text messages, or even in-person meetings. Adapt to the preferences of your occupants to ensure they receive and respond to your messages promptly.

Provide regular updates: Keep occupants informed about any property management or maintenance-related activities. Send regular updates on upcoming repairs, renovations, or service interruptions. This will help them plan accordingly and minimize any inconvenience.

Respond promptly: Be responsive to occupant inquiries, complaints, or requests. Acknowledge their messages in a timely manner and provide a clear timeline for addressing their concerns.

Prompt responses demonstrate your commitment to their satisfaction.

Use a friendly and professional tone: Maintain a courteous and professional tone in all communications. Address occupants by their names and use polite language. This helps create a positive and respectful atmosphere, promoting better relationships.

98

Provide detailed instructions: When giving instructions to occupants regarding property upkeep or maintenance, be specific and provide step-by-step guidelines if necessary.

This ensures clarity and reduces the likelihood of misunderstandings.

Seek feedback: Encourage occupants to provide feedback on their living experience or any concerns they may have. This feedback can help identify areas for improvement and show occupants that their opinions are valued.

Document communication: Keep a record of all communication with occupants, including dates, topics discussed, and any actions taken. This documentation can serve as a reference in case of any disputes or misunderstandings in the future.

Use visual aids: In certain cases, it may be helpful to use visual aids such as diagrams, photos, or videos to illustrate maintenance procedures or explain property-related matters.

Visual aids can enhance understanding and reduce confusion.

Respect privacy and confidentiality. Maintain the privacy and confidentiality of occupants' personal information.

99

Ensure that any sensitive information shared during communication is handled securely and in accordance with data protection regulations.

Remember, effective communication is a two-way process.

Actively listen to the concerns and feedback of occupants, and strive to find mutually beneficial solutions. By fostering open and transparent communication, you can promote positive relationships with occupants and enhance the overall property management experience.

Dealing with Tenants and Lease Agreements Introduction:

Dealing with tenants and lease agreements is an essential aspect of property management and real estate rental.

Establishing clear and mutually beneficial relationships with tenants while ensuring compliance with legal obligations is crucial for a successful and stress-free rental experience.

This note provides a comprehensive guide on how to effectively handle tenants and lease agreements, covering key aspects such as tenant screening, lease agreement creation, ongoing communication, and dispute resolution.

100

Tenant Screening:

a. Advertising: Advertise the rental property through various channels, such as online listings, local newspapers, or real estate agencies, to attract potential tenants.

b. Application Process: Develop a standardized tenant application form that collects necessary information such as personal details, rental history, employment information, and references.

c. Background Checks: Conduct thorough background checks, including credit history, criminal records, and employment verification, to ensure the suitability and reliability of potential tenants.

d. References: Contact previous landlords and personal references provided by the applicant to gain insights into their rental history and character.

Lease Agreement Creation:

a. Legal Assistance: Seek legal advice or consult a qualified attorney to draft a comprehensive lease agreement that complies with local rental laws and regulations.

b. Key Terms: Include important details in the lease agreement, such as rent amount, payment due dates, lease duration, security deposit requirements, utility responsibilities, pet policies, and maintenance obligations.

101

c. Rights and Responsibilities: Clearly outline the rights and responsibilities of both the landlord and tenant, including rules regarding property use, maintenance and repairs, noise restrictions, and other relevant provisions.

d. Addendums: Attach any additional addendums to the lease agreement that address specific concerns or requirements, such as smoking policies, parking regulations, or shared utility arrangements.

Ongoing Communication:

a. Timely and Clear Communication: Establish effective communication channels with tenants, ensuring that you promptly respond to their queries, concerns, and repair requests.

b. Rent Collection: Clearly communicate the rent payment process, due dates, and acceptable payment methods.

Consider implementing online payment options for convenience.

c. Regular Inspections: Conduct periodic inspections of the rental property to assess its condition and identify any maintenance or repair needs. Provide tenants with advance notice before entering the premises as required by local laws.

d. Renewals and Terminations: Initiate discussions with tenants regarding lease renewals or terminations well in advance to allow for proper planning and negotiation.

102

Maintenance and Repairs: a. Prompt Response: Address maintenance and repair requests promptly and efficiently. Establish a system for tenants to report issues and keep a record of all requests and their resolution.

b. Emergency Procedures: Clearly communicate emergency contact information and procedures to tenants for situations such as water leaks, power outages, or other urgent repairs.

c. Routine Maintenance: Schedule regular maintenance activities, such as HVAC system checks, gutter cleaning, or pest control, to ensure the property remains in good condition.

d. Tenant Responsibilities: Outline the responsibilities of tenants regarding minor maintenance tasks, such as replacing light bulbs, regularly changing air filters, or maintaining cleanliness.

Dispute Resolution:

a. Mediation: Encourage open communication and attempt to resolve disputes amicably through mediation or negotiation before considering legal action.

b. Legal Procedures: Familiarize yourself with local laws and regulations regarding eviction processes and follow them diligently if conflicts cannot be resolved through negotiation.

103

c. Documentation: Maintain detailed records of all interactions, communications, and incidents related to disputes or conflicts. These records may serve as valuable evidence if legal action becomes necessary.

Conclusion:

Effectively dealing with tenants and lease agreements requires careful attention to detail, clear communication, and adherence to legal obligations. By implementing a thorough tenant screening process, creating comprehensive lease agreements, maintaining open lines of communication, 104

CHAPTER SEVEN

Tax Strategies for Real Estate Investors Introduction:

Real estate investing offers numerous opportunities for wealth creation and portfolio diversification. However, understanding the tax implications and utilizing effective tax strategies can significantly impact an investor's overall profitability.

This note provides a comprehensive overview of tax strategies specifically tailored for real estate investors. By implementing these strategies, investors can maximize their tax benefits and optimize their investment returns.

Proper Entity Structure:

Choosing the right entity structure is crucial for real estate investors. Options include sole proprietorships, partnerships, limited liability companies (LLCs), S corporations, and real estate investment trusts (REITs). Each entity type has distinct tax implications and benefits, such as liability protection, pass-through taxation, and flexibility in managing properties.

Investors should consult with a tax professional to determine the most advantageous structure for their specific circumstances.

105

Depreciation:

Depreciation allows investors to deduct the cost of their property over time, reducing taxable income. Residential properties are typically depreciated over 27.5 years, while commercial properties are depreciated over 39 years.

However, utilizing cost segregation studies, investors can identify components of the property that can be depreciated over shorter periods, accelerating tax deductions and increasing cash flow.

1031 Exchange:

A 1031 exchange, also known as a like-kind exchange, allows investors to defer capital gains taxes when selling one property and reinvesting the proceeds in another similar property. By satisfying specific IRS requirements, investors can defer tax liabilities, preserve capital for future investments, and build wealth over time. It is essential to work with a qualified intermediary and adhere to strict timelines and guidelines to successfully execute a 1031

exchange.

Passive Losses and Rental Properties:

Rental property losses can often be classified as passive losses, which are subject to limitations under the tax code.

However, real estate professionals who actively participate in 106

rental activities or qualify as real estate professionals under IRS rules may be able to offset passive losses against other income, reducing overall tax liability. Meeting specific criteria and keeping thorough records are essential to substantiate real estate professional status.

Capital Gains and Losses:

When selling an investment property, investors incur capital gains or losses. By carefully timing sales, investors can strategically manage their tax liabilities. For example, offsetting capital gains with capital losses can reduce the amount of tax owed. Additionally, holding properties for more than one year qualifies them for long-term capital gains rates, which are typically lower than ordinary income tax rates.

Qualified Business Income (QBI) Deduction: The Tax Cuts and Jobs Act introduced the QBI deduction, which allows eligible taxpayers to deduct up to 20% of their qualified business income from pass-through entities, including rental real estate activities. To qualify, certain income and expense thresholds must be met, and the rental activity must rise to the level of a trade or business. Real estate investors should consult with a tax advisor to determine eligibility and optimize this deduction.

107

Utilizing Tax Credits: Investors should explore tax credits available for real estate investments, such as the Low-Income Housing Tax Credit (LIHTC) or the Historic Rehabilitation Tax Credit. These credits can offset tax liabilities on a dollar-for-dollar basis, reducing overall tax obligations while supporting socially beneficial investments. Engaging with tax professionals experienced in these credits is crucial to ensure compliance and maximize their benefits.

Self-Directed IRAs and 401(k)s:

Investors can utilize self-directed IRAs or 401(k)s to invest in real estate. This strategy offers potential tax advantages, such as tax-deferred or tax-free growth of investments.

However, complex rules and restrictions apply, and investors must ensure compliance with IRS regulations, including prohibited transaction rules and unrelated business taxable income (UBTI) provisions.

UNDERSTANDING REAL ESTATE TAXATION

Introduction:

108

Real estate taxation is a vital aspect of the real estate industry and plays a significant role in local and national economies.

This comprehensive note aims to provide a clear understanding of real estate taxation, including its purpose, types, calculation methods, and implications for property owners and governments. By grasping the fundamentals of real estate taxation, individuals can make informed decisions and effectively navigate the complexities of this field.

Purpose of Real Estate Taxation:

Real estate taxation serves multiple purposes, such as: a. Revenue Generation: Taxes on real estate properties contribute to government revenue and fund public services, infrastructure development, and essential amenities.

b. Property Ownership Regulation: Taxation can influence property ownership patterns, discourage property speculation, and promote more efficient land use.

c. Wealth Redistribution: Progressive taxation can be implemented to redistribute wealth by imposing higher tax rates on more valuable properties, ensuring a fairer distribution of resources.

Types of Real Estate Taxes:

109

There are various types of real estate taxes imposed by governments:

a. Property Taxes: Property taxes are the most common form of real estate taxation. They are assessed on the value of a property and are typically levied annually by local governments. The tax rate is determined based on the property's assessed value.

b. Transfer Taxes: Transfer taxes are incurred when ownership of a property is transferred from one party to another. These taxes are usually calculated as a percentage of the property's sale price or fair market value.

c. Capital Gains Taxes: Capital gains taxes are applicable when a property is sold at a profit. The tax is levied on the capital gain, which is the difference between the purchase price and the selling price of the property.

d. Inheritance and Estate Taxes: Inheritance and estate taxes may be imposed on real estate properties passed down through inheritance or as part of an estate. The tax rates and thresholds vary among jurisdictions.

Calculating Property Taxes:

110

Property taxes are calculated using various methods, depending on the jurisdiction:

a. Assessment-Based: Property taxes can be determined based on the assessed value of the property, which is usually conducted by a local government authority. The assessed value may consider factors like property size, location, construction quality, and recent sales of comparable properties.

b. Millage Rates: Millage rates are used to calculate property taxes based on a predetermined rate per thousand dollars of assessed value. The tax amount is determined by multiplying the assessed value by the millage rate.

c. Tax Exemptions and Deductions: Certain jurisdictions offer exemptions or deductions that reduce the taxable value of a property. These may include homestead exemptions for primary residences, exemptions for seniors or veterans, or deductions for energy-efficient improvements.

Implications for Property Owners:

Real estate taxation has several implications for property owners:

a. Financial Considerations: Property taxes form a significant part of homeownership costs, and property owners need to 111

budget for these expenses. Failure to pay property taxes can result in penalties, interest, or even foreclosure.

b. Market Value Impact: Property taxes can influence the market value of a property. High taxes may lower property values, while low taxes can attract buyers and increase demand.

c. Tax Planning: Property owners can engage in tax planning strategies to minimize their tax liabilities, such as taking advantage of applicable exemptions, deductions, or deferring capital gains taxes through 1031 exchanges.

Government Revenue and Services:

Real estate taxation plays a crucial role in funding government services, including:

a. Local Services: Property taxes are primarily used to finance local government services such as schools, police and fire departments, parks, road maintenance, and sanitation services.

b. Infrastructure Development: Tax revenues are utilized for infrastructure projects like building and maintaining roads, bridges, public transportation, water and sewage systems.

112

MAXIMIZING TAX BENEFITS AND DEDUCTIONS

Introduction:

Maximizing tax benefits and deductions is an essential strategy for individuals and businesses to minimize their tax liabilities and maximize their after-tax income. By understanding and utilizing the various tax benefits and deductions available, taxpayers can legally reduce their taxable income, thereby saving money and optimizing their overall financial situation.

This comprehensive note aims to provide an overview of key tax benefits and deductions, along with strategies to maximize their use.

I. **Understanding Tax Benefits:**

Tax Credits:

a. Definition: Tax credits directly reduce the amount of tax owed.

b. Types of tax credits:

Child Tax Credit

Earned Income Tax Credit

113

Education Tax Credits (American Opportunity Credit, Lifetime Learning Credit)

Renewable Energy Tax Credits

c. Strategies to maximize tax credits: Review eligibility criteria and requirements Keep records and receipts

Consult with a tax professional

Tax-Advantaged Accounts:

a. Definition: These accounts offer tax benefits for specific purposes.

b. Examples of tax-advantaged accounts: Individual Retirement Accounts (IRAs)

401(k) Plans

Health Savings Accounts (HSAs)

Flexible Spending Accounts (FSAs)

c. Strategies to maximize tax-advantaged accounts: Contribute the maximum allowed amount

Take advantage of employer matching contributions Use tax-advantaged accounts for eligible expenses II. Maximizing Deductions:

Standard Deduction vs. Itemized Deductions: a. Standard Deduction:

114

Applies to taxpayers who do not itemize deductions Amount varies based on filing status

b. Itemized Deductions:

Allow taxpayers to deduct specific expenses Examples of itemized deductions:

Medical expenses

State and local taxes

Mortgage interest

Charitable contributions

c. Strategies to maximize deductions:

Compare the standard deduction to potential itemized deductions

Consider timing strategies (bunching deductions) Keep proper documentation and receipts Above-the-Line Deductions:

a. Definition: Deductions subtracted from gross income to determine adjusted gross income (AGI).

b. Examples of above-the-line deductions: Educator expenses

Student loan interest

Health savings account contributions

c. Strategies to maximize above-the-line deductions: Be aware of eligible deductions

Keep accurate records

115

III. Additional Strategies: Tax Planning and Timing:

a. Evaluate income sources and timing of receipts b. Consider deferring or accelerating income or expenses c. Monitor tax law changes and plan accordingly Business Tax Deductions:

a. Understand deductions specific to business expenses b. Keep detailed records and separate personal and business expenses

c. Consult with a tax professional for guidance Charitable Contributions:

a. Donate to qualified charitable organizations b. Keep receipts and documentation for deductions c. Consider donating appreciated assets for additional tax benefits

Conclusion:

Maximizing tax benefits and deductions is a critical aspect of personal and business finance. By understanding the various tax credits, tax-advantaged accounts, and deductions available, individuals and businesses can optimize their tax positions and ultimately increase their after-tax income. It is 116

important to stay informed about changes in tax laws, consult with tax professionals, and maintain accurate records to fully benefit from available tax incentives. Implementing effective tax planning strategies will help individuals and businesses achieve their financial goals while remaining compliant with tax regulations.

Structuring Investments for Tax Efficiency Introduction:

Structuring investments for tax efficiency is a crucial aspect of financial planning and wealth management. By strategically organizing investments, individuals and businesses can minimize their tax liabilities and maximize their after-tax returns.

We will provide an overview of key strategies and considerations for structuring investments in a tax-efficient manner.

Asset Location:

One of the primary approaches to tax-efficient investing is asset location, which involves allocating different types of investments across various account types based on their tax 117

characteristics. The goal is to place investments in the most tax-efficient accounts to minimize overall tax liability.

a. Taxable Accounts: Investments held in taxable accounts are subject to capital gains taxes and dividend taxes.

Tax-efficient strategies for taxable accounts include investing in tax-efficient funds, utilizing tax-loss harvesting to offset gains with losses, and employing buy-and-hold strategies to defer capital gains taxes.

b. Tax-Advantaged Accounts: Tax-advantaged accounts such as individual retirement accounts (IRAs), 401(k)s, and 529

plans offer tax benefits that can help reduce the tax burden.

Strategies for tax-advantaged accounts include maximizing contributions, considering Roth conversions, and selecting investments with long-term growth potential.

Diversification and Asset Allocation: Proper diversification and asset allocation play a vital role in tax-efficient investing. By spreading investments across different asset classes, individuals can potentially reduce their tax exposure. It *is essential to consider the tax implications of each asset class and allocate investments accordingly.*

a. Tax-Efficient Investments: Certain investments generate more taxable income than others. For example, municipal 118

bonds provide tax-free interest income, making them attractive for taxable accounts. Similarly, tax-efficient mutual funds or ETFs can minimize taxable distributions.

b. Tax-inefficient Investments: Investments that generate regular income, such as high-yield bonds or real estate investment trusts (REITs), are better suited for tax-advantaged accounts to defer tax liabilities. These investments generate taxable income that can be sheltered within tax-advantaged accounts.

Tax-Loss Harvesting:

Tax-loss harvesting involves selling investments that have experienced a loss to offset taxable gains. By strategically harvesting losses, investors can reduce their tax liability.

However, it is important to adhere to IRS guidelines regarding wash sales, which prevent investors from repurchasing substantially identical securities within a 30-day period.

Capital Gains Management:

Managing capital gains is essential for long-term tax efficiency. Timing the realization of capital gains can have a significant impact on an investor's tax liability. Strategies for managing capital gains include:

a. Holding Period: Investments held for more than one year qualify for long-term capital gains tax rates, which are generally lower than short-term rates. Consider the holding period before selling investments to take advantage of the lower tax rates.

b. Gift and Estate Planning: Transferring appreciated assets as gifts or incorporating them into estate planning can help minimize capital gains taxes, especially if the recipient falls into a lower tax bracket.

Retirement Account Strategies:

Retirement accounts offer valuable tax advantages, and specific strategies can enhance their tax efficiency: a. Tax Deferral: Contributions to traditional retirement accounts, such as IRAs and 401(k)s, are typically tax-deductible, allowing for tax-deferred growth until withdrawal during retirement when tax rates may be lower.

b. Roth Conversions: Converting traditional retirement accounts into Roth IRAs can be advantageous, especially when tax rates are low. Roth IRAs offer tax-free growth and tax-free withdrawals in retirement.

120

Conclusion:

Structuring investments for tax efficiency is a complex but critical aspect of financial planning. By employing strategies such as asset location, diversification, tax-loss harvesting, capital gains management, and retirement account strategies, individuals and businesses can optimize their after 121

CHAPTER EIGHT

Long-Term Wealth Building and Exit Strategies Introduction:

Building long-term wealth is a goal shared by many individuals and businesses. It involves implementing strategies and making informed decisions over an extended period to accumulate assets, increase net worth, and achieve financial stability. An essential aspect of long-term wealth building is having exit strategies in place, which allow for a smooth transition or withdrawal from investments or business ventures.

This topic will provide an overview of long-term wealth building and explore various exit strategies to consider.

I. **Long-Term Wealth Building:**

Set Clear Financial Goals:

Establish specific, measurable, achievable, relevant, and time-bound (SMART) financial goals.

Determine your desired level of wealth, timeline, and the assets or investments you wish to acquire.

122

Create a Comprehensive Financial Plan: Develop a well-defined financial plan that aligns with your goals.

Consider factors such as income, expenses, savings, investments, and risk tolerance.

Seek professional advice, if necessary, to ensure an effective plan.

Diversify Investments:

Allocate investments across various asset classes (e.g., stocks, bonds, real estate) to mitigate risk.

Regularly review and rebalance your portfolio to maintain diversification.

Take Advantage of Compounding:

Start saving and investing early to benefit from compounding returns over time.

Reinvest dividends, interest, or capital gains to accelerate wealth growth.

Manage Risk:

Understand and assess the risks associated with different investment options.

Consider diversifying across industries, geographic regions, and investment types.

123

Regularly review and update your risk management strategy.

Maintain a Long-Term Perspective:

Avoid making impulsive investment decisions based on short-term market fluctuations.

Stay focused on your long-term financial goals and resist the temptation to time the market.

II. **Exit Strategies:**

Sale of Assets:

One common exit strategy is to sell assets, such as real estate properties, stocks, or businesses.

Timing the sale strategically can maximize returns.

Consider tax implications and seek professional advice to optimize the transaction.

Initial Public Offering (IPO):

Businesses with substantial growth potential may consider going public through an IPO.

This exit strategy allows owners to sell shares to the public and unlock liquidity.

IPOs require careful planning, compliance with regulations, and engaging investment banks.

124

Merger or Acquisition: Selling a business or merging with another company can be an exit strategy.

Evaluate potential acquirers or merger partners that align with your business objectives.

Seek legal and financial advice to negotiate favorable terms and ensure a smooth transition.

Succession Planning:

For business owners, succession planning involves transferring ownership and management control.

Identify and groom potential successors, whether within the family or the organization.

Develop a clear plan and communicate it effectively to stakeholders.

Transition to Passive Income:

Consider shifting from active income to passive income streams, such as rental properties or investments with regular dividends.

Build a portfolio that generates consistent income to replace or supplement active income.

Estate Planning:

125

Estate planning ensures the smooth transfer of assets upon retirement or death.

Establish wills, trusts, and powers of attorney to protect your wealth and provide for future generations.

Consult legal and financial professionals to create a comprehensive estate plan.

Conclusion:

Long-term wealth building requires discipline, strategic planning, and a focus on your financial goals. By diversifying investments, managing risk, and leveraging the power of compounding, you can accumulate wealth over time. Additionally, having well-defined exit strategies is crucial to transition smoothly from investments or business **BUILDING EQUITY AND APPRECIATION**

Introduction:

Building equity and appreciation are crucial components of wealth creation and financial growth. Whether it's in the context of real estate, investments, or businesses, understanding how to build equity and appreciate assets is essential for long-term financial success.

126

We will delve into the concept of equity, discuss strategies for building equity and appreciation, and highlight their significance in wealth accumulation.

I. Understanding Equity:

Equity refers to the ownership value or interest that an individual or entity holds in an asset after subtracting any outstanding liabilities. In simpler terms, it represents the net worth or value of an asset that belongs to the owner. Equity can be built and increased over time through various means.

II. Building Equity:

A. Real Estate:

Property Ownership: Owning real estate is a common way to build equity. As you make mortgage payments, a portion goes toward reducing the principal amount owed, thus increasing your equity in the property.

Appreciation: Real estate properties can appreciate in value over time, leading to an increase in equity. Factors such as market conditions, location, and property improvements can influence appreciation.

B. Investments:

127

Stock Market: Investing in stocks can generate equity over time. By purchasing shares of a company, you become a partial owner and can benefit from capital appreciation if the stock price increases.

Mutual Funds and Exchange-Traded Funds (ETFs): These investment vehicles allow investors to pool their money into diversified portfolios of stocks, bonds, or other assets. As the underlying investments appreciate, the value of your investment increases, resulting in equity growth.

C. Businesses:

Business Ownership: Owning a business allows you to build equity as the enterprise grows. By reinvesting profits into the business or attracting investors, the value of your ownership stake can increase.

Business Expansion: Expanding operations, entering new markets, or developing new products/services can lead to increased revenues and higher business valuation, thereby building equity.

III. Appreciating Assets:

Appreciation refers to the increase in value or worth of an asset over time. While equity can be built through various means, appreciation represents the passive growth of an asset's value, often influenced by market forces or other external factors.

128

A. Real Estate:

Market Demand: Favorable market conditions, such as increasing demand for housing, can drive property values up, resulting in appreciation.

Home Improvements: Making strategic upgrades and renovations to a property can enhance its value, leading to appreciation.

B. Investments:

Economic Factors: Economic growth, industry performance, and market trends can cause the value of stocks, bonds, and other investments to appreciate.

Dividends and Interest: Some investments provide regular income in the form of dividends or interest payments, which contribute to overall appreciation.

C. Businesses:

Competitive Advantage: Developing a unique product or service, building a strong brand, and establishing a loyal customer base can contribute to the appreciation of a business.

129

Scalability: A business with scalable operations and the potential for expansion can experience increased value and appreciation over time.

IV. Significance of Equity and Appreciation: A. Wealth Accumulation: Building equity and experiencing asset appreciation are fundamental to accumulating wealth and achieving financial independence.

B. Leverage and Borrowing: Equity can be leveraged for borrowing purposes, allowing individuals and businesses to access capital at favorable rates based on the value of their assets.

C. Retirement Planning: Building equity in real estate, investments, and businesses can provide a solid foundation for retirement savings and generate passive income streams.

D. Generational Wealth: Equity and asset appreciation can be passed down to future generations, creating a legacy of financial stability and opportunities.

Conclusion:

Building equity and appreciating assets are vital strategies for long-term

Strategies for Selling or Exiting Investments 130

Introduction:

Selling or exiting investments is an important aspect of investment management. Whether you are an individual investor or a business owner, knowing when and how to sell or exit an investment is crucial for maximizing returns and minimizing risks.

We will explore various strategies for selling or exiting investments that can help you make informed decisions and achieve your financial goals.

Define Your Investment Objectives:

Before considering selling or exiting an investment, it is essential to clearly define your investment objectives. Are you looking for short-term gains or long-term growth? Are you aiming for income generation or capital appreciation?

Understanding your goals will provide a framework for determining the appropriate timing and method for selling or exiting your investments.

Regular Monitoring and Review:

Regularly monitoring and reviewing your investment portfolio is vital for identifying opportunities to sell or exit investments. Keep a close eye on market conditions, industry trends, and the performance of individual assets. Conduct 131

periodic reviews to assess whether your investments are aligning with your objectives and if any adjustments are necessary.

Fundamental Analysis:

Employ fundamental analysis to evaluate the intrinsic value of your investments. Assess the financial health, growth prospects, and competitive position of the underlying companies or assets. If you find that the fundamentals have deteriorated significantly or no longer support your investment thesis, it may be a sign that it's time to sell or exit the investment.

Technical Analysis:

Utilize technical analysis to study price patterns, market trends, and trading volumes of your investments. Technical indicators can provide insights into the momentum and strength of an investment. Sell signals such as moving average crossovers, trendline breaks, or overbought conditions may indicate a suitable time to exit a position.

Stop-Loss Orders:

Implementing stop-loss orders can help limit potential losses by automatically triggering a sale if an investment reaches a predetermined price level. Setting a stop-loss order ensures 132

that you have an exit strategy in place if the market turns against your position or if specific criteria are met. This strategy can provide protection and prevent emotional decision-making during market volatility.

Profit-Taking:

Consider taking profits when an investment has reached your target price or achieved substantial gains. By selling a portion of your holdings, you can secure profits and reduce your exposure to potential market downturns. This strategy allows you to lock in gains while still maintaining a position in the investment for further potential upside.

Rebalancing:

Rebalancing involves adjusting the allocation of your investment portfolio to maintain desired asset class weights.

Periodically review your portfolio's performance and asset allocation. If certain investments have outperformed and become overweighted, selling a portion of those investments and reallocating the proceeds to underperforming assets can help maintain a balanced and diversified portfolio.

Tax Considerations:

Take into account the tax implications of selling or exiting investments. Depending on your jurisdiction and the holding 133

period, capital gains taxes may apply. Consider consulting with a tax advisor to optimize your selling strategy, such as utilizing tax-efficient accounts or timing sales to minimize tax liabilities.

Market Timing:

Attempting to time the market perfectly can be challenging and risky. Rather than trying to predict short-term market movements, focus on your long-term investment goals and the fundamentals of the investments. Avoid making impulsive decisions based on short-term market fluctuations and maintain a disciplined approach to selling or exiting investments.

Seek Professional Advice:

When in doubt or when dealing with complex investment scenarios, it is advisable to seek professional advice.

Financial advisors, portfolio managers, or investment professionals can provide guidance tailored to your specific circumstances and goals. They can assist in evaluating investment opportunities, determining appropriate exit strategies, and optimizing your overall investment portfolio.

Conclusion:

134

Selling or exiting investments requires careful consideration and analysis.

1031 Exchanges and Other Tax-Advantaged Exits A 1031 exchange is a tax-deferred exchange under Section 1031 of the Internal Revenue Code (IRC) that allows individuals and businesses to defer capital gains taxes when they sell certain types of property and reinvest the proceeds into like-kind replacement property. This exchange is named after the specific section of the tax code that governs it. In addition to 1031 exchanges, there are other tax-advantaged exits that individuals and businesses can consider.

We will explore 1031 exchanges and briefly touch upon some other tax-advantaged strategies.

1031 Exchanges:

A 1031 exchange provides a way to defer the payment of capital gains taxes when selling an investment property by reinvesting the proceeds into another qualifying property.

Here are key points to understand:

135

a. Like-Kind Property: The property being sold and the replacement property must be of like-kind. Like-kind refers to the nature or character of the property, not its quality or grade. For example, a residential rental property can be exchanged for a commercial property or vacant land.

b. Timeline: To qualify for a 1031 exchange, the taxpayer must adhere to specific timelines. The taxpayer must identify potential replacement properties within 45 days of selling the original property and complete the exchange by acquiring the replacement property within 180 days.

c. Qualified Intermediary (QI): A QI is a third-party facilitator who helps oversee the exchange process. The QI holds the proceeds from the sale of the original property and ensures they are used to acquire the replacement property.

d. Tax Deferral: By completing a 1031 exchange, the taxpayer can defer the payment of capital gains taxes that would otherwise be due upon the sale of the original property. The taxes are deferred until the replacement property is sold without being exchanged further.

136

e. Boot: If there is any cash or non-like-kind property received in the exchange, it is referred to as "boot." Boot is taxable to the extent of gain realized or cash received.

Other Tax-Advantaged Exits:

In addition to 1031 exchanges, there are other strategies that can provide tax advantages for individuals and businesses looking to exit or reposition their investments. Here are a few examples:

a. Opportunity Zones: Opportunity Zones were established under the Tax Cuts and Jobs Act of 2017 to encourage investment in economically distressed communities.

Investors can defer and potentially reduce capital gains taxes by investing their realized capital gains into Qualified Opportunity Funds (QOFs) that invest in designated Opportunity Zones.

b. Delaware Statutory Trusts (DSTs): A DST is a legal entity that allows multiple investors to own fractional interests in real estate without the need for active management. By investing in a DST, investors can potentially defer capital gains taxes and enjoy passive income from the property.

137

c. Installment Sales: An installment sale allows the seller to spread the recognition of capital gains over multiple tax years by receiving the sale proceeds in installments over time. This strategy can help reduce the immediate tax burden and provide the opportunity to defer taxes.

d. Charitable Remainder Trusts (CRTs): A CRT is a tax-exempt trust that allows an individual to donate appreciated assets (such as real estate) to the trust and receive income from the trust for a specified period. By donating the property to the CRT, the individual can potentially receive a charitable tax deduction and avoid immediate capital gains taxes.

e. Conservation Easements: By donating a conservation easement, which is a legal agreement to limit development on a property, an individual can potentially receive significant tax deductions. This strategy is often used by landowners to preserve environmentally or historically significant land.

138

CHAPTER NINE

OVERCOMING CHALLENGES AND RISKS

Introduction:

Real estate investment is a popular avenue for wealth creation due to its potential for long-term appreciation and income generation. However, like any investment, it comes with its fair share of challenges and risks.

This chapter aims to outline some common challenges and risks associated with real estate investing and provide strategies for overcoming them, ultimately maximizing the potential for building wealth in this sector.

Market Volatility:

Real estate markets can experience periods of volatility, influenced by factors such as economic downturns, interest rate fluctuations, and regulatory changes. To overcome this challenge:

a. Conduct thorough market research: Stay informed about market trends, local economic conditions, and future development plans to make informed investment decisions.

139

b. Diversify your portfolio: Invest in multiple properties across different locations and property types to mitigate the impact of market volatility.

c. Focus on long-term goals: Real estate investment is a long-term strategy. Don't get swayed by short-term market fluctuations and stick to your investment plan.

Financing and Cash Flow:

Obtaining financing for real estate investments can be challenging, especially for new investors. Additionally, managing cash flow effectively is crucial to sustain and grow your real estate wealth. Consider the following strategies: a. Build a good credit score: Maintain a strong credit history to improve your chances of obtaining favorable financing terms.

b. Network with financial institutions: Develop relationships with banks, credit unions, and private lenders to explore financing options tailored to your needs.

c. Conduct thorough financial analysis: Assess the potential cash flow of a property before purchasing, accounting for expenses, vacancies, and maintenance costs. This analysis ensures you have sufficient income to cover expenses and generate a profit.

Property Management:

140

Managing properties can be time-consuming and challenging, especially if you own multiple units or properties in different locations. To overcome property management challenges:

a. Hire a professional property management company: Delegate day-to-day tasks such as tenant screening, rent collection, and property maintenance to experienced professionals.

b. Leverage technology: Utilize property management software and online platforms to streamline communication, rent collection, and maintenance requests.

c. Build a reliable team: If managing properties independently, establish relationships with reliable contractors, plumbers, electricians, and other professionals who can assist with repairs and maintenance.

Legal and Regulatory Compliance:

Real estate investments are subject to various legal and regulatory requirements, including zoning laws, tenant rights, and taxation. To navigate these challenges: a. Consult with legal professionals:

Seek advice from real estate attorneys who specialize in local laws and regulations to ensure compliance and minimize legal risks.

b. Stay updated on changes: Keep abreast of legal and regulatory changes that could impact your real estate 141

investments through industry publications, networking, and professional organizations.

Market Saturation and Competition:

In popular real estate markets, competition can be fierce, leading to inflated prices and reduced profit margins. Here's how to overcome market saturation:

a. Seek emerging markets: Look for areas experiencing growth and development potential that offer better investment opportunities.

b. Be patient and diligent: Conduct thorough due diligence on potential properties, negotiate prices, and wait for the right investment opportunity that aligns with your investment goals.

c. Differentiate your property: Consider property renovations or unique selling points to attract tenants and buyers in a competitive market.

Conclusion:

Real estate wealth creation can be a rewarding endeavor, but it is not without its challenges and risks. By conducting comprehensive market research, managing finances and cash flow effectively, utilizing professional property management, adhering to legal and regulatory requirements, and adapting to market conditions, investors can overcome these 142

challenges and mitigate risks, ultimately maximizing their potential for success in real estate investment. Remember that prudent decision-making, patience, and a long-term perspective are crucial

Market Fluctuations and Economic Downturns in Real Estate Investment

Introduction:

Real estate investment is subject to various market fluctuations and economic downturns that can significantly impact investment returns and property values.

Understanding these fluctuations and downturns is crucial for investors to make informed decisions and mitigate potential risks.

This chapter provides an overview of market fluctuations and economic downturns in real estate investment, including their causes, effects, and strategies for navigating through challenging times.

I. **Market Fluctuations:**

143

Definition:

Market fluctuations refer to the periodic changes in real estate market conditions, such as property prices, rental rates, demand, and supply.

Causes of Market Fluctuations:

a. Economic factors: Economic indicators such as GDP

growth, inflation, interest rates, and employment levels influence the demand for real estate.

b. Market speculation: Speculative activities, such as excessive buying or selling based on anticipated price movements, can create artificial market fluctuations.

c. Supply and demand dynamics: Changes in population, demographics, and housing preferences can affect the supply and demand balance, leading to market fluctuations.

d. Government policies: Legislative changes, zoning regulations, tax incentives, and subsidies can impact real estate market conditions.

Effects of Market Fluctuations:

a. Property values: Fluctuations can cause property values to rise or fall, impacting investor returns and equity.

b. Rental income: Market fluctuations can affect rental rates, resulting in changes to cash flow and potential rental vacancies.

144

c. Financing availability: Lenders' willingness to provide loans and interest rates can fluctuate based on market conditions, affecting investment opportunities.

Strategies for Dealing with Market Fluctuations: a. Diversification: Investing in different types of properties or markets can help reduce exposure to localized market fluctuations.

b. Long-term perspective: Adopting a long-term investment strategy can help weather short-term market volatility.

c. Thorough research: Conducting extensive market research and due diligence can identify potential market fluctuations and inform investment decisions.

d. Active management: Implementing proactive property management practices, such as maintaining competitive rental rates and adapting to market changes, can mitigate the impact of fluctuations.

II. Economic Downturns:

Definition:

Economic downturns, also known as recessions or economic contractions, refer to periods of significant decline in economic activity, often characterized by reduced GDP

growth, increased unemployment, and financial instability.

145

Causes of Economic Downturns: a. Business cycles: Economic downturns are a natural part of the business cycle, which consists of alternating periods of expansion and contraction.

b. Financial crises: Events such as banking crises, stock market crashes, or housing market collapses can trigger severe economic downturns.

c. External shocks: Global events like pandemics, geopolitical conflicts, or natural disasters can disrupt economies and lead to downturns.

Effects of Economic Downturns on Real Estate Investment: a. Declining property values: Economic downturns often lead to reduced demand, oversupply, and decreased property values.

b. Rental market challenges: High unemployment rates can affect tenants' ability to pay rent, leading to increased vacancies and rental income declines.

c. Financing difficulties: Economic downturns can make it more challenging to secure financing due to tighter lending standards and reduced investor confidence.

Strategies for Navigating Economic Downturns: 146

a. Cash reserves: Maintaining adequate cash reserves can help cover expenses and mortgage payments during periods of reduced cash flow.

b. Focus on stable markets: Investing in stable markets with diversified economic bases and strong fundamentals can provide resilience during economic downturns.

c. Value-add opportunities:

During an economic downturn, businesses face challenges in maintaining profitability and sustainability. However, there are several value-add opportunities that can help organizations navigate these difficult times. Here are some strategies to consider:

Diversification of product/service offerings: Explore new markets, develop innovative products, or expand your service portfolio. Diversifying your offerings can help mitigate the impact of a downturn in one sector or market.

Focus on customer retention: In challenging economic times, customer loyalty becomes crucial. Enhance your customer service, offer loyalty programs, and provide personalized experiences to retain existing customers. Satisfied customers are more likely to stay with you and refer your business to others.

147

Cost optimization and efficiency: Review your business operations and identify areas where costs can be reduced without compromising quality. Streamline processes, negotiate better deals with suppliers, and eliminate unnecessary expenses. Increasing efficiency can improve your bottom line.

Strategic partnerships and collaborations: Seek opportunities for strategic partnerships with complementary businesses.

Collaborating with other organizations can help you expand your customer base, share resources, and reduce costs. Look for win-win collaborations that can add value to both parties involved.

Focus on innovation and R&D: Invest in research and development to foster innovation. Identify emerging trends and technologies that align with your business, and develop new products or services that meet evolving customer needs.

Innovation can give you a competitive advantage and open new revenue streams.

Market expansion and internationalization: Explore new geographical markets or consider expanding your business internationally. While this strategy requires careful planning 148

and research, entering new markets can provide growth opportunities and diversify your revenue streams.

Enhance marketing and communication efforts: During a downturn, it's important to maintain brand visibility and effectively communicate with your target audience. Invest in marketing campaigns, leverage digital channels, and optimize your messaging to reach and engage potential customers.

Focus on talent development: Invest in your employees'

skills and knowledge to enhance productivity and efficiency.

Offer training programs, provide opportunities for professional growth, and promote a positive work culture.

Engaged and skilled employees can contribute significantly to your organization's success.

Explore alternative financing options: During economic downturns, traditional financing may become more challenging to obtain. Explore alternative financing options such as crowdfunding, peer-to-peer lending, or government grants to secure the necessary capital for growth or operational needs.

149

Maintain financial discipline and contingency planning: Implement strong financial management practices, including regular financial analysis, cash flow monitoring, and scenario planning. Having contingency plans in place can help you respond effectively to unexpected challenges and mitigate potential risks.

Remember, every business is unique, and the suitability of these strategies may vary depending on your industry, market conditions, and organizational goals. It's important to assess your specific situation and adapt these strategies accordingly to maximize their effectiveness in navigating an economic downturn.

Legal and Regulatory Considerations in Real Estate Investment

Real estate investment involves the acquisition, ownership, management, rental, or sale of property for the purpose of generating income or appreciation. Like any investment, real estate comes with legal and regulatory considerations that investors need to be aware of to ensure compliance and protect their interests.

150

Overview of the key legal and regulatory considerations in real estate investment.

Property Acquisition:

a. Title Search: Conducting a thorough title search is essential to verify ownership, any liens, encumbrances, or legal disputes associated with the property.

b. Purchase Agreement: A legally binding contract should be drafted and signed by both parties, outlining the terms and conditions of the property purchase.

Financing:

a. Mortgage Laws: Understanding mortgage laws and regulations, including interest rates, loan-to-value ratios, and repayment terms, is crucial for financing real estate investments.

b. Loan Documentation: Proper documentation, such as promissory notes and mortgages, should be executed to secure the loan and protect the lender's interests.

Zoning and Land Use:

a. Zoning Regulations: Familiarize yourself with local zoning regulations and ensure that the property's intended use aligns with the designated zoning classification.

151

b. Land Use Restrictions: Some properties may have restrictions on land use due to conservation or historical preservation requirements. Compliance with these restrictions is important to avoid legal issues.

Property Management:

a. Lease Agreements: Clearly drafted lease agreements protect the rights of both landlords and tenants, outlining the terms of occupancy, rent, maintenance responsibilities, and dispute resolution mechanisms.

b. Fair Housing Laws: Complying with fair housing laws ensures that tenants are not discriminated against based on factors such as race, religion, gender, or disability.

c. Health and Safety Regulations: Adhering to local health and safety regulations is vital to providing a habitable and safe environment for tenants.

Taxation:

a. Property Taxes: Understanding property tax laws and regulations is crucial to budgeting and managing real estate investments effectively.

b. Income Taxes: Rental income from real estate investments is subject to income tax. Familiarize yourself with tax laws and consider consulting a tax professional to optimize tax planning.

152

Environmental Considerations: a. Environmental Regulations: Properties may be subject to environmental regulations, including assessments for contamination, hazardous materials, or protected habitats.

Compliance with these regulations is essential to avoid legal liabilities.

Insurance and Liability:

a. Property Insurance: Adequate property insurance coverage protects against risks such as damage, theft, or liability claims from third parties.

b. Liability Protection: Structuring real estate investments through limited liability entities (e.g., LLCs) can provide personal liability protection for investors.

Real Estate Market Regulations:

a. Real Estate Licensing: Some jurisdictions require real estate agents or brokers to be licensed. Ensure compliance with licensing regulations when engaging in real estate transactions.

b. Disclosure Requirements: Sellers and landlords are often obligated to disclose certain property information to buyers or tenants. Familiarize yourself with disclosure requirements to avoid legal disputes.

153

Dispute Resolution:

a. Alternative Dispute Resolution: Consider including clauses in contracts that require parties to engage in alternative dispute resolution methods, such as mediation or arbitration, to resolve conflicts without litigation.

b. Legal Representation: In the event of legal disputes or complex transactions, seeking legal representation from real estate attorneys with expertise in property law is advisable.

It is important to note that this overview provides general guidance and is not exhaustive. Real estate laws and regulations can vary significantly between jurisdictions.

Therefore, it is essential to consult with legal professionals specializing in real estate law and stay updated with local regulations when investing in real estate **Mitigating Investment Risks in Real Estate Investment**

Introduction:

Real estate investment can be a lucrative opportunity for investors, but it is not without risks. Understanding and 154

mitigating these risks is crucial to protecting your investment and maximizing returns.

Comprehensive overview of key strategies and considerations for mitigating investment risks in real estate.

Conduct Thorough Due Diligence:

Before investing in any real estate property, it is essential to conduct thorough due diligence. This includes researching the property, its location, market trends, and potential risks.

Engage professionals such as real estate agents, appraisers, and lawyers to ensure accurate and reliable information.

Evaluate Market Conditions:

Assessing the current and future market conditions is crucial.

Analyze supply and demand dynamics, vacancy rates, rental trends, and economic indicators in the area. This information helps identify potential risks and determine the viability and profitability of the investment.

Diversify Your Portfolio:

Diversification is a fundamental risk mitigation strategy.

Avoid investing all your capital in a single property or market segment. Instead, spread your investments across different types of real estate, such as residential, commercial, industrial, or geographic locations. Diversification helps 155

minimize the impact of localized market downturns or specific property risks.

Perform Comprehensive Financial Analysis: Conduct a thorough financial analysis of the property before making an investment decision. Evaluate factors such as cash flow projections, operating expenses, potential rental income, and financing options. Consider working with a financial professional or analyst to ensure accurate calculations and informed decision-making.

Maintain Sufficient Liquidity:

Real estate investments often require significant capital and have long holding periods. It is crucial to maintain sufficient liquidity to cover unexpected expenses, mortgage payments, and periods of vacancy. Having reserves ensures that you can weather potential financial challenges without jeopardizing the investment or resorting to distress sales.

Consider Property Insurance:

Insurance plays a vital role in mitigating risks associated with real estate investments. Obtain comprehensive property insurance coverage to protect against unforeseen events such as natural disasters, fire, vandalism, or liability claims.

156

Consult with insurance experts to assess the appropriate coverage based on the property type and location.

Stay Informed about Legal and Regulatory Matters: Real estate investments are subject to various legal and regulatory requirements. Stay informed about zoning regulations, building codes, permits, and other legal considerations. Engage legal professionals to review contracts, lease agreements, and ensure compliance with local laws. Understanding and adhering to these regulations mitigates the risk of penalties, fines, or legal disputes.

Build a Reliable Network:

Developing a strong network of real estate professionals, including property managers, contractors, and realtors, is invaluable. Trusted partners can provide valuable insights, advice, and support during the investment lifecycle.

Additionally, having a reliable network helps mitigate risks associated with property management, maintenance, and tenant-related issues.

Monitor and Adapt to Market Changes:

Real estate markets are dynamic and subject to fluctuations.

Regularly monitor market trends, rental rates, and property values to identify potential risks or opportunities. Stay 157

informed about economic factors, demographic changes, and other external influences that may impact the property's performance. Adapt your investment strategy accordingly to mitigate risks and capitalize on market shifts.

Exit Strategies:

Before entering a real estate investment, have a clear exit strategy in mind. Define your investment horizon and consider options such as selling, refinancing, or converting the property into another use. Having a well-thought-out exit plan allows you to proactively manage potential risks and optimize returns.

Conclusion:

Real estate investments offer attractive opportunities, but they also carry inherent risks. By following these strategies and considerations, investors can mitigate risks, make informed decisions, and safeguard their investments.

158

159

160